1000
ATOMIC BOMB MISSILES AGAINST WITCHCRAFT AND EVIL ALTARS

Warfare Prayers to Uproot Evil Patterns, Shatter Witchcraft, Silence the Devil, and Release Your Destiny

"Thou shalt not suffer a witch to live."
—Exodus 22:18 (KJV)

Evangelist Tracy C. Moonga

Healing Minister | Intercessor | Fire-Prophetic Voice | End-Time Warrior

Gospel Songwriter | Worshipper | Revival Sound Carrier

Soul-Winner with a Divine Assignment to Populate Heaven and Depopulate Hell.

Copyright & Rights

© **2025** Tracy C. Moonga. All rights reserved. No part of this publication may be reproduced, transmitted, stored in a retrieval system, or shared in any form or by any means—whether photocopying, electronic, recording, or otherwise—without the prior written permission of the author.

Unauthorized reproduction, distribution, or transmission is strictly prohibited unless authorized by the Author of this book.

ENDORSEMENT & REVIEW

"This book is not just powerful—it is necessary."

1000 Atomic Bomb Missiles Against Witchcraft and Evil Altars is a spiritual warfare arsenal forged in fire. Evangelist Tracy C. Moonga has given the Body of Christ one of the most targeted, scripture-rich, and no-mercy prayer manuals of this generation.

Each missile is more than a prayer—it's a legal weapon, a prophetic strike, and a Holy Ghost-loaded declaration. These prayers were born in the trenches of midnight warfare, and they carry the anointing to break bondages, uproot evil altars, silence witchcraft, and recover stolen destinies.

If you are tired of delay, repeated affliction, strange dreams, or spiritual oppression—this book will transform your altar and set your fire back ablaze. It's not for spectators. It's for warriors.

Whether you're an intercessor, deliverance minister, or desperate believer, this manual will become your lifelong companion for daily warfare, family deliverance, and spiritual revival.

you will not remain the same.

You will not leave this book empty.

This is your fire-loaded manual for total victory.

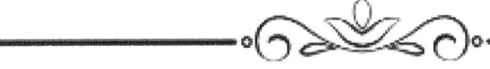

Dedication

This book is dedicated to the Holy Spirit, my Teacher, Fire, and Deliverer—without whom this assignment would not exist.It is also dedicated to every warrior, intercessor, family, and believer across the nations—not only in Africa—who is rising in boldness to confront witchcraft, altars, curses, and spiritual wickedness. May these atomic bomb missiles empower you to pray until the enemy flees.

MESSAGE FROM THE AUTHOR: This is not an ordinary book. This is not for spectators. This is for spiritual warriors. For those who are tired of demonic interference, patterns of delay, and witchcraft oppression.These are atomic bomb missiles—targeted warfare prayers forged in fire and backed by the Word of God. This manual is for those who are ready to cry out until something breaks. Get into the war zone.Don't sit down to pray—stand, pace, roar, and strike!

Pray daily. Pray in the midnight hour. Pray in night vigils.

Fast as led by the Holy Spirit.Praise for at least 10 minutes before you begin the warfare.

Repeat each prayer 3 times or more until you feel peace, breakthrough, or release before you go to the next prayer.

Don't move to the next prayer until you know something has shifted.

This book can be used by individuals, families, pastors, intercessors, and deliverance ministers. It can be prayed on behalf of others—stand in the gap, and let fire fall.

Pray like Elijah. War like Jehu. Strike like David. Roar like Jesus.

WHO SHOULD USE THIS BOOK

This book is not for the faint of heart. It is for those who are ready to rise, war, and win.

Use this book if:

You are facing repeated attacks, spiritual delay, sickness, or patterns that don't break.

You've been targeted by witchcraft, evil altars, ancestral bondage, or territorial strongholds.

You feel stuck—nothing is moving, and you know there's a spiritual cause.

You've had dreams of eating, sex, serpents, animal attacks, or dark altars.

You are an intercessor, prayer warrior, or deliverance minister.

You're praying for your spouse, children, family, ministry, or community.

You feel tormented, oppressed, or trapped in emotional, marital, or financial warfare.

You are tired of delay, tired of silence, tired of affliction— and you're ready to fight.

This book is your spiritual war hammer.

Your altar of fire.

Your manual for vengeance and victory.

Whether you're praying for yourself or standing in the gap for others—this is your time.

Warrior, pray until something breaks.

Let's begin.

SPIRITUAL ACTIVATION: Begin with 10 Minutes Praise, Thanksgiving, and Repentance

Before launching the 1000 Atomic Bomb Missiles, follow this spiritual protocol to ignite divine presence and ensure fire falls on your altar.

1. Praise and Thanksgiving

Enter His Gates
(Psalm 100)

"Enter into His gates with thanksgiving, and into His courts with praise. Be thankful unto Him, and bless His name." – Psalm 100:4

Spend at least 10 minutes praising God aloud. Sing, dance, clap, or declare His goodness. You can use the 50 praise declarations provided in this book or simply speak from your heart. Praise silences the enemy and invites God's glory.

2. Repentance Prayer

Cleanse Before Fire (Psalm 51)

"Create in me a clean heart, O God; and renew a right spirit within me." – Psalm 51:10

Pray this before engaging in any warfare. This clears legal grounds and ensures your altar is not defiled.

Repentance Prayer:

Heavenly Father, I come before You with a humble heart. Have mercy on me, O God, according to Your unfailing love. According to Your great compassion, blot out my transgressions.

Wash me thoroughly from my iniquity. Cleanse me from every sin, pride, lust, rebellion, unforgiveness, bitterness, spiritual laziness, disobedience, and fear.

Create in me a clean heart, O God, and renew a right spirit within me. Cast me not away from Your presence. Restore unto me the joy of Your salvation, and uphold me with Your Spirit.

Let the Blood of Jesus cleanse my heart, mind, hands, and motives. I repent for every known and unknown sin—spoken, thought, or acted upon. I stand under the Blood of Jesus. I plead for mercy. In Jesus' name. Amen.

Now that you've praised and repented, you are spiritually ready.

Your altar is clean. Your heart is aligned. Your voice is activated.

Let the 1000 Atomic Bomb Missiles begin.

50 POINTS OF PRAISE AND WORSHIP TO EXALT GOD AND JESUS (WITH SCRIPTURE)

1.

I praise You, O Lord, for You are the Alpha and the Omega—there is no one like You.

(Revelation 22:13)

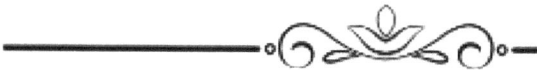

2.

I worship You, Jesus, the Lamb of God who takes away the sins of the world.

(John 1:29)

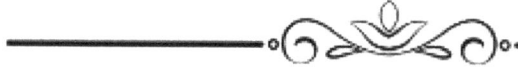

3.

I exalt You, Yahweh, for You are my refuge and fortress.

(Psalm 91:2)

4.
I praise You, Jehovah Jireh, for You are my provider.

(Genesis 22:14)

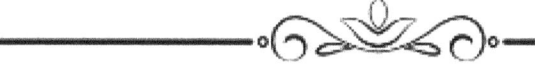

5.
I glorify You, Lord, for Your steadfast love never ceases.

(Lamentations 3:22-23)

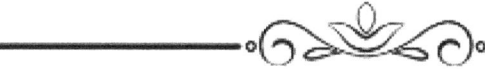

6.
I worship You, El Elyon, Most High God—none can compare to You.

(Genesis 14:18-20)

7.
I magnify You, Lord Jesus, for Your blood speaks better things than the blood of Abel.

(Hebrews 12:24)

8.
I adore You, Holy Spirit, my Teacher, my Comforter, my Fire.

(John 14:26)

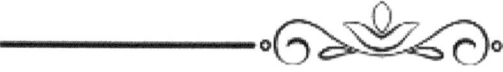

9.
I bless You, O God, for You are the King of glory, strong and mighty.

(Psalm 24:8)

10.
I exalt You, Lord of Hosts, for the battle belongs to You.

(1 Samuel 17:47)

11.
I lift Your name, Jehovah Shalom, my peace in every storm.

(Judges 6:24)

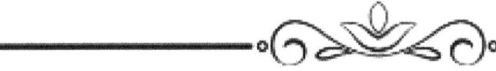

12.
I praise You, Jesus, the resurrection and the life.

(John 11:25)

13.
I worship You, Adonai, the Lord and Master of all.

(Psalm 8:1)

14.
I glorify You, Emmanuel, for You are God with us.

(Matthew 1:23)

15.
I magnify You, El Shaddai, the all-sufficient One.

(Genesis 17:1)

16.
I honor You, Lord, for You are clothed in majesty and light.

(Psalm 104:1-2)

17.
I exalt You, Jesus, my Redeemer and Deliverer.

(Job 19:25)

18.
I praise You, Jehovah Nissi, my banner of victory.

(Exodus 17:15)

19.
I bless You, Father, for You are worthy of all praise and adoration.

(Psalm 145:3)

20.
I glorify Your name, O Lord, for Your name is a strong tower.

(Proverbs 18:10)

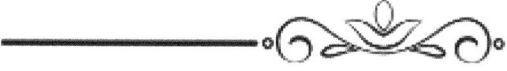

21.
I worship You, the Ancient of Days, seated upon the throne.

(Daniel 7:9-10)

22.

I praise You, God of Abraham, Isaac, and Jacob—the covenant-keeping God.

(Exodus 3:6)

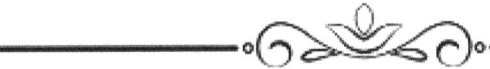

23.

I honor You, Jesus, the Lion of the Tribe of Judah.

(Revelation 5:5)

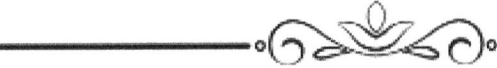

24.

I magnify You, O God, for You are holy, holy, holy.

(Isaiah 6:3)

25.
I adore You, the Bright and Morning Star.

(Revelation 22:16)

26.
I praise You, Lord, for You inhabit the praises of Your people.

(Psalm 22:3)

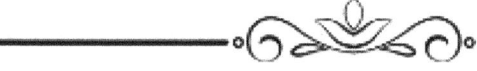

27.
I worship You, the Light of the world—You shine in darkness.

(John 8:12)

28.
I glorify You, the Good Shepherd who lays down His life for the sheep.

(John 10:11)

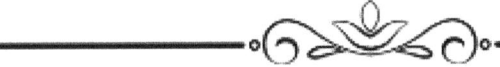

29.
I exalt You, Father, for You are faithful even when we are faithless.

(2 Timothy 2:13)

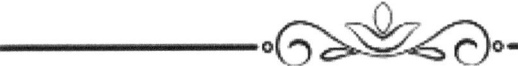

30.
I praise You, Jesus, for You are the way, the truth, and the life.

(John 14:6)

31.
I honor You, O God, who was, who is, and who is to come.

(Revelation 1:8)

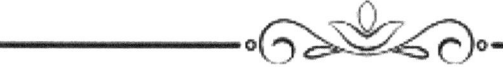

32.
I worship You, my Creator and Sustainer.

(Colossians 1:16-17)

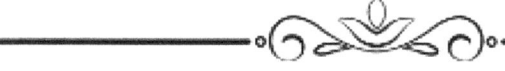

33.
I bless Your holy name, for You are slow to anger and rich in love.

(Psalm 103:8)

34.
I glorify You, the Righteous Judge who rules with justice.

(Psalm 9:7-8)

35.
I exalt You, Jesus, the Word made flesh.

(John 1:14)

36.
I praise You, the Rock of Ages—immovable and unshakable.

(Isaiah 26:4)

37.
I magnify You, O Lord, for You are gracious and full of compassion.

(Psalm 145:8)

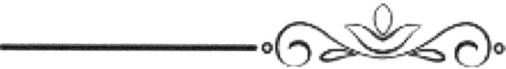

38.
I worship You, Father of lights, from whom every good gift comes.

(James 1:17)

39.
I adore You, the Lord who heals me.

(Exodus 15:26)

40.
I honor You, Jesus, who makes all things new.

(Revelation 21:5)

41.
I glorify You, the Commander of the army of the Lord.

(Joshua 5:14)

42.
I praise You, King of kings and Lord of lords.

(Revelation 19:16)

43.

I bless You, Jesus, for You conquered death, hell, and the grave.

(1 Corinthians 15:55-57)

44.

I magnify You, Father, for You never sleep nor slumber.

(Psalm 121:4)

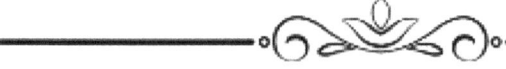

45.

I exalt You, the God who answers by fire.

(1 Kings 18:24)

46.
I worship You, the I AM THAT I AM.

(Exodus 3:14)

47.
I glorify You, my Defender and Shield.

(Psalm 3:3)

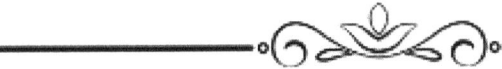

48.
I praise You, the Author and Finisher of my faith.

(Hebrews 12:2)

49.
I honor You, God of wonders, who does great and mighty things.

(Jeremiah 32:17)

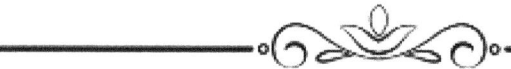

50.
I declare: To You alone belongs all glory, honor, power, and dominion forever and ever. Amen!

(Revelation 5:13)

SECTION ONE: REPENTANCE AND CONSECRATION MISSILES

(PRAYERS 1–30)

1.
O Lord my God, I come before You in repentance—have mercy on me and cleanse me from every known and unknown sin.

Scripture: Psalm 51:1-2

2.
Blood of Jesus, wash my hands, my mouth, and my thoughts—purify me and make me a vessel of warfare and power.

Scripture: 1 John 1:7

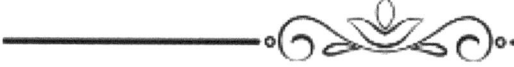

3.
Father, I renounce every covenant I knowingly or unknowingly entered into with darkness. I break it now by the Blood of Jesus.

Scripture: Colossians 1:13-14

4.

O Lord, let every legal ground Satan is using against me be destroyed by mercy and the fire of Your judgment.

Scripture: Romans 8:1-2

5.

I surrender every area of my life to the Holy Spirit. Fill me afresh and reign in every dimension of my destiny.

Scripture: Galatians 5:16

6.

Blood of Jesus, speak on my behalf in the courts of Heaven. Silence every voice of accusation by divine mercy.

Scripture: Hebrews 12:24

7.
I plead the Blood of Jesus over my name, my record, my bloodline—let the Blood cancel every evil charge against me.

Scripture: Revelation 12:11

8.
I renounce the sins of my ancestors—every inherited guilt, I break free by the Blood of Jesus.

Scripture: Lamentations 5:7

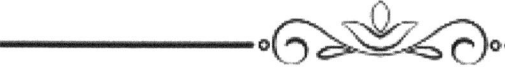

9.
Lord, anything in me that attracts demonic attack, expose and purge it now by fire.

Scripture: Malachi 3:2-3

10.

I forgive every person who has wounded me, cursed me, or betrayed me. I release them and cut all soul ties in Jesus' name.

Scripture: Matthew 6:14

11.

O Lord, let the refining fire of the Holy Ghost burn through me now—make me a battle-ready weapon.

Scripture: Isaiah 4:4

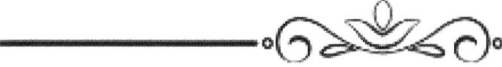

12.

Father, I rededicate my body, soul, and spirit to You—let Your fire possess me completely.

Scripture: Romans 12:1

13.
Any unrepented doorway I opened to the enemy—through sin, fear, or ignorance—I shut it now by the Blood of Jesus.

Scripture: Ephesians 4:27

14.
I disconnect myself from every ungodly soul tie, spiritual marriage, or demonic attachment—be cut off by fire.

Scripture: 2 Corinthians 6:14-17

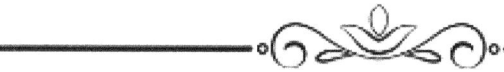

15.
O Lord, deliver me from self-sabotage and secret bondage—I renounce them now.

Scripture: John 8:36

16.

Let the altar of holiness be rebuilt in my life. I declare, I am set apart for fire and warfare.

Scripture: 2 Timothy 2:21

17.

I call on the Blood of Jesus to cover my foundation, my past, my roots—redeem me from every ancestral defilement.

Scripture: Galatians 3:13

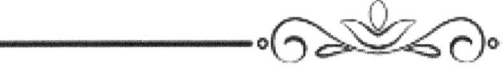

18.

Holy Spirit, release fresh oil upon me for war—revive my prayer altar and stir prophetic boldness in me.

Scripture: Acts 1:8

19.

Every curse of limitation activated by sin or disobedience—I cancel it by repentance and by the Blood of Jesus.

Scripture: Deuteronomy 28:1-2

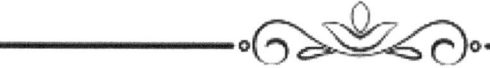

20.

Lord Jesus, anoint me afresh with boldness, purity, and spiritual aggression—let my tongue become a weapon.

Scripture: Psalm 144:1

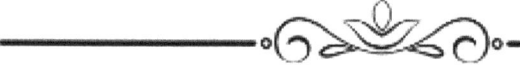

21.

I strip myself of every filthy garment, spiritual laziness, and lukewarmness—let the fire of revival consume me.

Scripture: Zechariah 3:3-4

22.

O God, let this consecration provoke angelic warfare on my behalf—dispatch warring angels now!

Scripture: Psalm 34:7

23.

By the Blood of Jesus, I shut every demonic gateway opened through dreams, trauma, or exposure—be sealed now!

Scripture: Isaiah 22:22

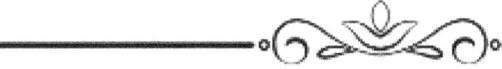

24.

Father, let every unclean appetite, hidden rebellion, and secret addiction be burned out by the fire of God.

Scripture: Titus 2:11-12

25.

I plead the Blood of Jesus upon my mind—I reject double-mindedness, confusion, and emotional instability.

Scripture: 2 Timothy 1:7

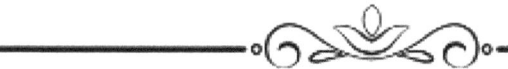

26.

Lord, rewire my emotions, my memories, and my personality—let the fire of Your Spirit sanctify my soul.

Scripture: 1 Thessalonians 5:23

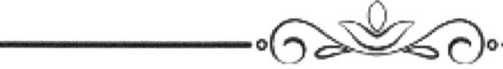

27.

I break every unconscious agreement I made with pain, fear, poverty, or bondage—I revoke it by the Blood of Jesus.

Scripture: Matthew 18:18

28.
O Lord, sanctify my words, my thoughts, and my motives—make me Your battle axe.

Scripture: Jeremiah 51:20

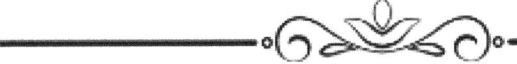

29.
I declare, I belong to Jesus. I am a weapon of war. I am a holy vessel. I am a firebrand.

Scripture: 2 Corinthians 10:4

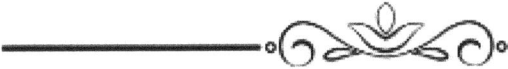

30.
Father, receive me as a living sacrifice and make me ready for spiritual battle without fear or apology.

Scripture: Romans 12:1-2

SECTION TWO: MISSILES TO DESTROY WITCHCRAFT ALTARS

(PRAYERS 31–60)

31.
Every witchcraft altar raised to control my destiny, I release atomic judgment against you—scatter by fire and the Blood of Jesus!

Scripture: Deuteronomy 7:5

32.
O God arise, let thunder and lightning from Heaven strike every altar of manipulation speaking against my rising.

Scripture: Psalm 18:13-14

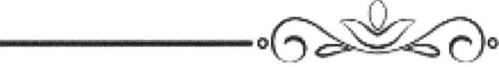

33.
I invoke the fire in the Blood of Jesus against every evil altar where my name, photo, or garments have been placed—burn now!

Scripture: Leviticus 6:13

34.

Every satanic priest fueling altars of affliction against my life—collapse and perish by the vengeance in the Blood of Jesus!

Scripture: Isaiah 49:26

35.

Altars of delay and limitation built by household enemies—scatter beyond repair by the Blood of Jesus and Holy Ghost fire!

Scripture: Psalm 27:2

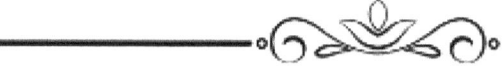

36.

Any family member invoking my name on ancestral altars—be silenced permanently by the fire of God!

Scripture: Micah 7:6

37.
Every witchcraft altar calling for blood sacrifice from my family—be soaked in the Blood of Jesus and destroyed without recovery!

Scripture: Exodus 12:13

38.
Altars of poverty and stagnation erected in my village or lineage—catch fire and scatter to ashes!

Scripture: Judges 6:25

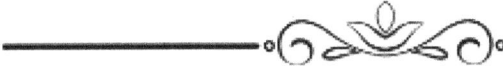

39.
I speak confusion into every coven or gathering fueling altars against my health and breakthrough—scatter by the Blood!

Scripture: Psalm 68:1

40.

Evil altars assigned to cage my womb, my marriage, or my calling—break by thunder and by the Blood of Jesus!

Scripture: Jeremiah 1:10

41.

I release atomic bomb missiles into the marine altars working against my progress—be uprooted by Holy Ghost fire!

Scripture: Isaiah 27:1

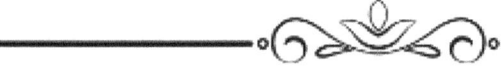

42.

Every tree of witchcraft planted around my house or compound, receive the axe of God—be cut down and burned to ashes!

Scripture: Matthew 3:10

43.
I command fire from Heaven to fall upon every shrine where my name is under surveillance—let those powers be wasted now!

Scripture: 1 Kings 18:38-40

44.
By the Blood of Jesus, I nullify every incantation, sacrifice, and spell activated on any altar against me.

Scripture: Numbers 23:23

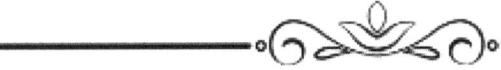

45.
Every hidden altar in my family house crying for my downfall—O God arise, scatter them with no mercy!

Scripture: Isaiah 54:15

46.
Let the voice of the Blood of Jesus silence the voice of every wicked altar working against my favor and open doors.

Scripture: Hebrews 12:24

47.
I disconnect my name, my image, and my records from every altar of tragedy and failure!

Scripture: Colossians 2:14

48.
Every altar demanding offerings of tears, losses, or premature death—be dismantled by the Blood of the Lamb!

Scripture: Psalm 102:20

49.

I plead the Blood of Jesus upon my family altar—let it be rebuilt with fire, purity, and divine encounters.

Scripture: Genesis 35:3

50.

Let every monitoring spirit stationed at an altar to monitor my steps be blinded and destroyed without recovery!

Scripture: 2 Kings 6:18

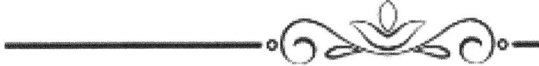

51.

Every altar summoning my name for evil rituals—backfire by fire! I shall not be used as a sacrifice!

Scripture: Ezekiel 13:18-19

52.

O Lord, let every altar of the serpent be set on fire by Holy Ghost atomic missiles—I crush every snake spirit now!

Scripture: Luke 10:19

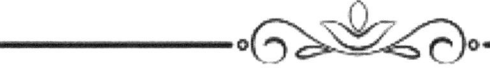

53.

I declare spiritual war against altars of delay in marriage, promotion, and purpose—scatter by the Blood of Jesus!

Scripture: Isaiah 10:27

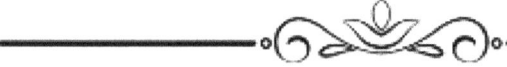

54.

Let thunder, fire, and the sword of judgment fall upon every hidden altar calling for vengeance against me or my lineage!

Scripture: Nahum 1:6

55.
Any demonic padlock placed on an altar to cage my progress—break now in the name of Jesus!

Scripture: Isaiah 22:22

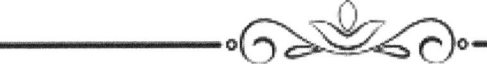

56.
Altars of midnight attacks and nightmares—be roasted by the fire of the Holy Spirit! I take back my sleep!

Scripture: Job 5:12-13

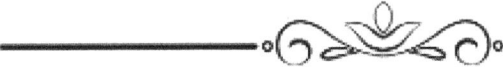

57.
I stand upon the Rock, Christ Jesus, and declare: every altar fighting my destiny be crushed and blown away!

Scripture: Matthew 21:44

58.
Let every altar of ancestral failure receive the atomic bomb of Heaven—be buried permanently!

Scripture: Galatians 3:13-14

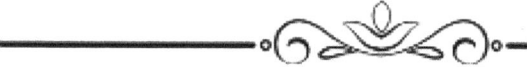

59.
O God arise, and let the fire of Elijah answer every battle altar confronting my household—let the wicked burn!

Scripture: 2 Kings 1:12

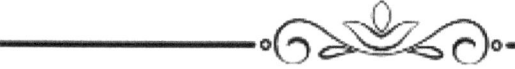

60.
I command all evil altars in my father's and mother's lineage to catch fire and die permanently—my destiny is released by the Blood of Jesus!

Scripture: Jeremiah 30:16-17

SECTION THREE: MISSILES TO SCATTER MONITORING SPIRITS AND EVIL SURVEILLANCE

(PRAYERS 61–90)

61.

Every spiritual drone assigned to track my movement, be consumed by the fire of Jehovah Sabaoth, the Lord of Hosts!

Scripture: Psalm 27:1-2

62.

O consuming fire, arise and devour every spiritual camera planted against my household—turn them into ashes!

Scripture: Hebrews 12:29

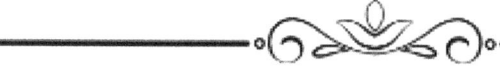

63.

Holy Ghost, explode like dynamite against every network of sorcery monitoring my marriage, finances, or anointing!

Scripture: Acts 1:8

64.

Every astral projector flying to report my progress—be electrocuted by the lightning of El Elyon, the Most High God!

Scripture: Luke 10:18-19

65.

By the Blood of Jesus, I disappear from every demonic radar—I become invisible to the kingdom of darkness!

Scripture: Colossians 3:3

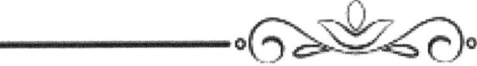

66.

I break every evil tracking system operating through dreams, shadows, or objects—be exposed and destroyed!

Scripture: Isaiah 8:10

67.

Every satanic screen showing my movements—receive fire from Jehovah Mekoddishkem, the Lord who sanctifies!

Scripture: Psalm 121:7

68.

I shut down every altar-powered surveillance channel watching my home—scatter by the power of Elohim!

Scripture: Psalm 18:13

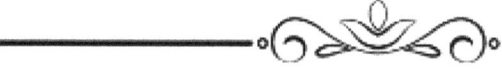

69.

I invoke the name of Jesus Christ, the Lion of Judah—roar against every witch or wizard spying on me in the spirit!

Scripture: Revelation 5:5

70.

Every evil observer from the pit of hell—fall into the pit you dug for me by the power of the Ancient of Days!

Scripture: Psalm 35:8

71.

O sword of the Lord, pursue and silence every familiar spirit reporting my affairs—let them be swallowed in darkness!

Scripture: Jeremiah 25:33

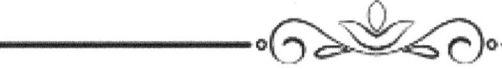

72.

I decree Holy Ghost fire around my children, my work, and my rising—every evil monitor, perish by thunder!

Scripture: Isaiah 54:17

73.

Let the voice of Jehovah Nissi—my Banner of Victory—scatter every demon assigned to delay my progress through observation!

Scripture: Exodus 17:15

74.

O Word of God, like a hammer, smash every evil screen, portal, and demonic lens used to watch me!

Scripture: Jeremiah 23:29

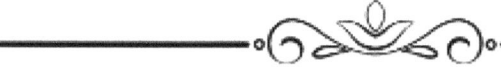

75.

I declare war against witchcraft satellites and spirit watchers—be grounded now by the name of Jesus Christ!

Scripture: Luke 10:19

76.

Holy Spirit, encrypt my life with divine fire—every spirit trying to decode my destiny, fail and be scattered!

Scripture: Proverbs 21:30

77.

I disconnect my image from every evil altar, mirror, water bowl, and charm—let them catch fire and scatter!

Scripture: Numbers 23:23

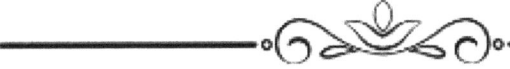

78.

O Blood of Jesus, cover my home, my gates, and my possessions—let no demon cross this line of fire!

Scripture: Revelation 12:11

79.
I evoke the presence of the Lord of Hosts—surround me with warrior angels that strike without mercy!

Scripture: Psalm 91:11-12

80.
Every network of spiritual espionage—scatter into confusion by the Blood of Jesus and the fire of Jehovah Tsabaoth!

Scripture: Psalm 68:1

81.
Let the thunder of Elohim break the hands of spiritual reporters—let their source of power dry up now!

Scripture: Psalm 29:3-5

82.

I speak the fire of Jehovah Rohi, my Shepherd, into every place where my name is being invoked in darkness!

Scripture: John 10:11

83.

O Jesus, Man of War, rise and wage battle against every dark surveillance and demonic spy—let them be consumed without mercy!

Scripture: Exodus 15:3

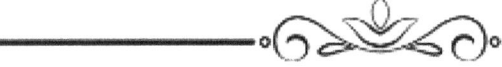

84.

I release divine confusion upon all my spiritual enemies—they will hear noise and scatter without touching me!

Scripture: 2 Kings 7:6

85.

Every chain of ancestral bondage tying me to the failures of my father's house—break now by the Blood of Jesus!

Scripture: Galatians 3:13

86.

I release the hammer of God to crush every foundational altar speaking against my rising—scatter by fire!

Scripture: Jeremiah 23:29

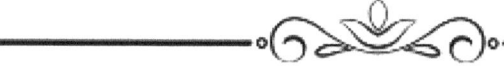

87.

O Lord, let every evil pattern running in my bloodline be arrested and reversed by the power in the name of Jesus!

Scripture: 2 Corinthians 5:17

88.
I plead the Blood of Jesus over my bloodline—no curse shall continue beyond me! I am the end of that evil line!

Scripture: Lamentations 5:7

89.
Every voice of my ancestors crying against my destiny—be silenced by the Blood of the eternal covenant!

Scripture: Hebrews 12:24

90.
I command every inherited yoke—be broken from my neck by the anointing of the Holy Ghost!

Scripture: Isaiah 10:27

SECTION FOUR: MISSILES TO BREAK ANCESTRAL CHAINS AND GENERATIONAL BONDAGE

(PRAYERS 91–120)

91.

O God, arise and deliver me from every family idol and its demands—let their power collapse forever!

Scripture: Deuteronomy 7:5

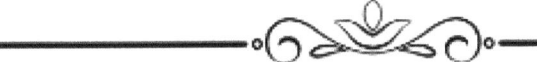

92.

I renounce every family covenant with darkness, poverty, delay, and stagnation—I enter the covenant of life in Christ!

Scripture: Isaiah 28:18

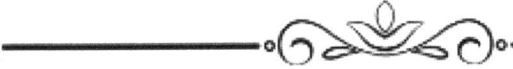

93.

Every generational spell cast on my name, womb, mind, or calling—expire now by Holy Ghost fire!

Scripture: Psalm 109:17-20

94.
Let the fire of the Holy Spirit trace and destroy every evil inheritance assigned to my generation!

Scripture: Ezekiel 18:2-4

95.
I declare: I shall not repeat the failures, afflictions, or errors of my ancestors—I am a new bloodline in Christ!

Scripture: 1 Peter 1:18-19

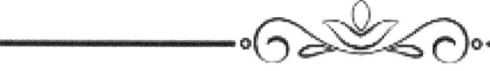

96.
O sword of fire, enter my foundation and cut off every spiritual chain passed from mother to child—be broken now!

Scripture: Isaiah 54:17

97.
Every curse of marital failure running through my family—catch fire and die by the Blood of Jesus!

Scripture: Numbers 23:8

98.
I command the spirit of untimely death, divorce, addiction, or insanity rooted in my bloodline—be consumed by fire!

Scripture: Psalm 118:17

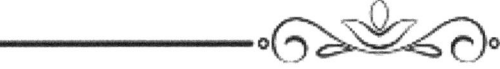

99.
Let every ancestral altar buried in my place of birth be exhumed and scattered by fire and the Blood of Jesus!

Scripture: Judges 6:25

100.
I disconnect from every spiritual chain linking me to the altars of witch doctors, herbalists, or false prophets!

Scripture: Deuteronomy 18:10-12

101.
O Blood of Jesus, erase every handwriting of bondage and evil pattern written against me from generations past!

Scripture: Colossians 2:14

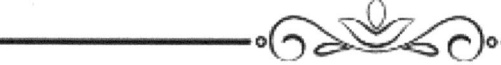

102.
Every satanic dedication done on my behalf as a child—I reverse it by the Blood of the Lamb and fire of God!

Scripture: Isaiah 49:24-26

103.
I command every generational affliction in my body, bones, or blood—dry up now by divine fire!

Scripture: Jeremiah 30:17

104.
By the power in the name of Jesus, I set my children free from every generational attack—no curse shall pass down!

Scripture: Psalm 112:2

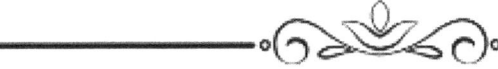

105.
I reject every evil transfer from my family history—my story shall be different, by the covenant of the Blood!

Scripture: Jeremiah 29:11

106.
Every chain of rising and falling in my lineage—break now, never return again!

Scripture: Proverbs 4:18

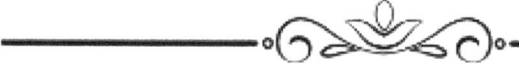

107.
I invoke the name of Jesus Christ to rewrite the story of my generation—we are free, healed, and blessed!

Scripture: Joel 2:25-26

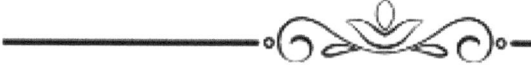

108.
Let the altar of Jesus Christ speak louder than every evil foundation laid by my forefathers!

Scripture: 1 Corinthians 3:11

109.

O Lord, destroy every record of failure and shame programmed into my generational code—rewrite it with fire!

Scripture: Zechariah 3:4

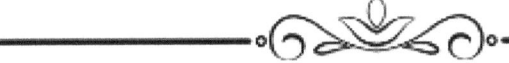

110.

I decree: from this day forward, my family shall be known for fire, favor, and breakthrough in Jesus' name!

Scripture: Isaiah 61:9

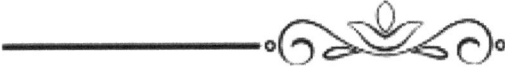

111.

Every satanic root feeding evil fruits into my destiny—dry up and die! I bear good fruit only!

Scripture: Matthew 3:10

112.

I uproot every demonic tree planted in my family line—be cast into the fire and never grow again!

Scripture: Matthew 15:13

113.

Let divine fire go back into my lineage and burn every hidden witchcraft seed trying to reproduce through me!

Scripture: Obadiah 1:17-18

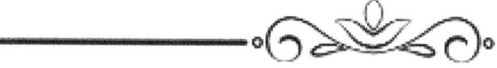

114.

I declare total freedom and covenant alignment for me and my household—by the Blood of Jesus and fire of God, we are delivered!

Scripture: Joshua 24:15

115.

O Lord of Hosts, arise with fire, thunder, and lightning—scatter every marine witchcraft network assigned to delay my breakthrough!

Scripture: Psalm 18:13-14

116.

I invoke the sword of the Lord to strike every water spirit operating through dreams, altars, and seduction—be slain now!

Scripture: Jeremiah 50:35

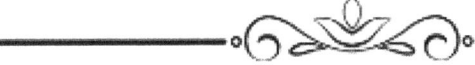

117.

Every marine covenant affecting my marriage, health, or finances—be broken by the Blood of Jesus Christ, the Covenant-Keeper!

Scripture: Zechariah 9:11

118.

O consuming fire, dry up every evil river, ocean, and spiritual reservoir empowering marine powers against me!

Scripture: Hebrews 12:29

119.

Jehovah El Gibbor, Man of War, thunder against the queen of the coast and her spiritual daughters—scatter them by holy terror!

Scripture: Isaiah 42:13

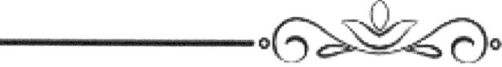

120.

Blood of Jesus, flow into every marine altar where my name is buried—let the foundation explode with fire!

Scripture: Revelation 12:11

SECTION FIVE: MISSILES AGAINST MARINE POWERS AND WATER SPIRITS

(PRAYERS 121–150)

Foundation Scripture:
"Thou shalt not suffer a witch to live."

– Exodus 22:18

121.

I release atomic bomb prayers into every marine kingdom holding my virtue—release it now by fire!

Scripture: Isaiah 49:25

122.

Every ring, gift, or token given in the spirit to tie me to water spirits—I reject and burn it by the fire of the Holy Ghost!

Scripture: Acts 19:19

123.

O Yahweh, King of Glory, enter the sea and dry it up—let every marine gate be shut by Your eternal authority!

Scripture: Nahum 1:4

124.
Every spiritual marriage rooted in the marine world—be annulled by the Blood of the Everlasting Covenant!

Scripture: Hebrews 13:20

125.
Let thunder from Jehovah Nissi destroy every hidden portal between my life and marine covens—no access permitted!

Scripture: Psalm 29:7

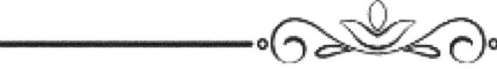

126.
By the name of Jesus Christ of Nazareth, I break every marine stronghold operating in my foundation—scatter without recovery!

Scripture: 2 Samuel 22:14-15

127.

I command the rod of judgment to strike every octopus spirit strangling my progress—be cut off now!

Scripture: Psalm 110:2

128.

O Lord Jesus, the Lion of Judah, roar against every serpent and dragon in the deep sent to monitor me—let them drown in fire!

Scripture: Psalm 74:13-14

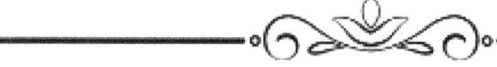

129.

I cast Holy Ghost grenades into the depths of the sea—every marine throne, be disarmed and dissolved!

Scripture: Job 26:12

130.

Let every seductive power from the marine world be disgraced—I shall not be manipulated by spirit spouses!

Scripture: Proverbs 6:25-26

131.

I plead the Blood of Jesus over my dreams—no more sexual attacks, water dreams, or defilement in the name of Yeshua!

Scripture: Matthew 5:8

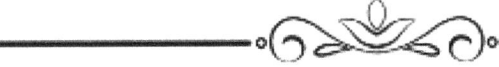

132.

Jehovah Mekoddishkem, sanctify my bed, my body, and my spiritual life from every marine pollution!

Scripture: Leviticus 20:7-8

133.

Let the whirlwind of Yahweh sweep away every marine agent assigned to my calling—no room for retreat!

Scripture: Jeremiah 23:19

134.

Every generational access point to the marine world—be closed by fire and sealed with the Blood of the Lamb!

Scripture: Isaiah 22:22

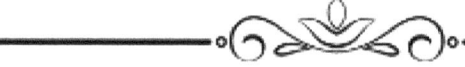

135.

O God arise, blow up every spiritual aquarium where my blessings have been caged—break it now in the name of Jesus!

Scripture: Jeremiah 51:20-21

136.
Sword of fire, arise and destroy every Leviathan spirit tormenting my family line—perish without escape!

Scripture: Isaiah 27:1

137.
I call on Jehovah Rohi—lead me beside still waters, not demonic ones! Guide me away from the traps of marine systems.

Scripture: Psalm 23:2

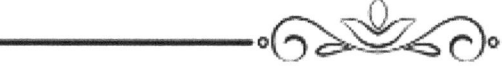

138.
Let every evil sea spirit that swore to never let me go be swallowed by the storm of Jehovah Tsabaoth!

Scripture: Psalm 144:6-7

139.

I reject every child, seed, or implant from the marine world—I am a seed of Abraham, covered by the Blood of Jesus!

Scripture: Galatians 3:29

140.

Holy Ghost torpedoes, target and explode every satanic submarine spirit hiding in the water realms—flush them out!

Scripture: Psalm 18:15

141.

I declare my life unpolluted, uncontaminated, and undefiled—I am covered by Jesus, my Deliverer and Redeemer!

Scripture: Ephesians 5:27

142.

O God of Elijah, arise with thunder and burn every marine scroll, contract, and record of my name—let them burn to ash!

Scripture: Deuteronomy 7:5

143.

I block every dream pipeline used by water spirits to re-enter my life—no access, no return, in the name of Jesus!

Scripture: Matthew 12:43-45

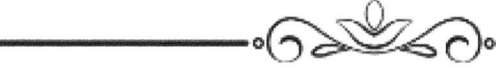

144.

I declare total victory over all marine forces—by the Blood of Jesus, the fire of God, and the name above all names—JESUS CHRIST!

Scripture: Philippians 2:10

145.

Every strongman in my foundation assigned to block my rising—fall down and die by the atomic judgment of God!

Scripture: Matthew 12:29

146.

I release the sword of the Lord against every ancient serpent hiding in my bloodline—be uprooted and destroyed by fire!

Scripture: Isaiah 27:1

147.

O consuming fire, locate every buried charm, sacrifice, or evil object tied to my name—be exposed and burnt to ashes!

Scripture: Deuteronomy 7:5

148.
Every familiar spirit dominating my family and enforcing patterns of failure—be cast into everlasting chains!

Scripture: Jude 1:6-7

149.
I speak destruction to every altar of premature death erected in my family—let the Blood of Jesus silence them forever!

Scripture: Psalm 118:17

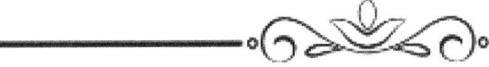

150.
O Lord, arise with thunder and lightning, and scatter every serpent crawling in my body—come out by fire without residue!

Scripture: Luke 10:19

SECTION SIX: MISSILES TO DESTROY STRONGMEN, CHARMS, ANCIENT SERPENTS & FAMILY BONDAGES (PRAYERS 151–180)

Foundation Scripture:

"Thou shalt not suffer a witch to live."

– Exodus 22:18

151.

Every spiritual padlock used to shut down my health or delay my destiny—break by the rod of iron!

Scripture: Revelation 2:27

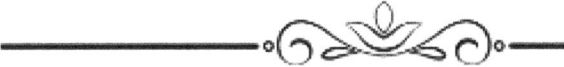

152.

Any demonic animal—serpent, dog, frog, bird, or rat—used to manipulate my life, catch fire and be roasted now!

Scripture: Leviticus 20:27

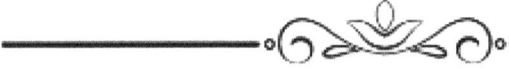

153.

I command every sickness hiding in my body, fed by witchcraft or generational altars—die from the root by the Blood of Jesus!

Scripture: Jeremiah 30:17

154.

Every foundational spirit sponsoring marital problems, poverty, and setbacks—be uprooted now by divine vengeance!

Scripture: Psalm 11:3

155.

By the name of Jesus Christ, I send missiles of fire into the graveyards where my destiny has been tied—be loosed now!

Scripture: Ezekiel 37:12

156.

O Sword of Fire, cut off every ancient pattern of delay, oppression, or affliction repeating through generations!

Scripture: Ecclesiastes 1:9

157.

I invoke the Blood of Jesus to erase every evil handwriting of inherited affliction over my life and my household!

Scripture: Colossians 2:14

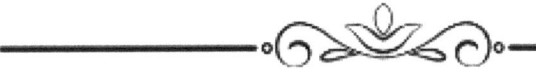

158.

I declare: I will not die young, I will not suffer what killed my mother or father—this curse is broken forever!

Scripture: Isaiah 65:20

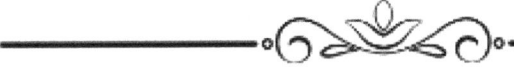

159.

O fire of God, enter into my bones, my bloodstream, my organs—burn out every satanic deposit and demonic serpent!

Scripture: Hebrews 12:29

160.
I disconnect my name and DNA from every evil family altar and demonic sacrifice—let there be total separation by fire!

Scripture: Romans 12:1-2

161.
Every ancestral python squeezing life out of my finances, health, and purpose—die by thunder!

Scripture: Acts 16:16-18

162.
Any sickness programmed into my body through dreams, food, or contact—be flushed out by the Blood of Jesus!

Scripture: Mark 16:18

163.
I reject every spiritual inheritance of depression, barrenness, stagnation, and shame—this pattern ends with me!

Scripture: Isaiah 61:7

164.
Every moving object in my body—whether serpent, worm, or charm—be electrocuted by Holy Ghost fire now!

Scripture: Matthew 15:13

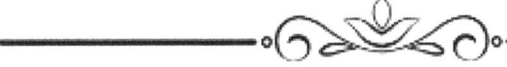

165.
I command the thunder of God to dismantle every altar demanding the blood of my family—be consumed by wrath!

Scripture: Ezekiel 21:1-3

166.

Every evil river flowing from my ancestral line into my life—dry up by the sword of Jehovah!

Scripture: Nahum 1:4

167.

O Lord, let the cry of the Blood of Jesus answer every affliction passed through my mother's womb—let it break!

Scripture: Revelation 12:11

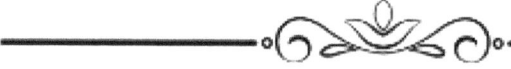

168.

I set fire to every family charm hidden in a shrine, forest, house, or grave—be scattered without remedy!

Scripture: Deuteronomy 12:3

169.

I break free from every satanic prediction, family prophecy, or evil name assigned to limit my future—scatter now!

Scripture: Isaiah 54:17

170.

O God of war, scatter every dark covenant renewed through bloodlines in my family—let fire fall on them!

Scripture: Judges 6:25

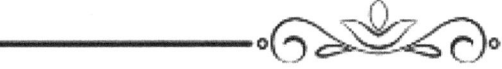

171.

Every chain of repetition—same sickness, same struggle, same delay—be broken now in Jesus' name!

Scripture: Nahum 1:9

172.

I declare war against premature death, terminal disease, and demonic hospital arrows—return to sender by thunder!

Scripture: Psalm 91:16

173.

I am delivered from generational suffering. I walk in divine exemption. I am a firebrand, and I belong to Jesus!

Scripture: Galatians 3:13

174.

Every witchcraft padlock used to lock my progress, break now by the rod of the Lord and scatter by fire!

Scripture: Isaiah 45:2

175.
I command every evil hand pressing pause on my destiny—wither now by thunder in the name of Jesus Christ!

Scripture: 1 Kings 13:4

176.
Altars of stagnation erected to trap my business, career, or ministry—catch fire and collapse beyond repair!

Scripture: Psalm 18:44-45

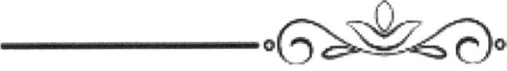

177.
O Lord, arise with your divine bulldozer and crush every demonic barrier resisting my movement forward!

Scripture: Micah 2:13

178.
I release atomic missiles into every stronghold of delay—scatter and release my testimony NOW!

Scripture: Daniel 10:12-13

179.
I declare war against premature death, terminal disease, and demonic hospital arrows—return to sender by thunder!

Scripture: Psalm 91:16

180.
Every financial devourer assigned to empty my purse, my account, and my harvest—be roasted without mercy!

Scripture: Malachi 3:11

SECTION SEVEN: MISSILES TO DISMANTLE DELAY, STAGNATION, AND FINANCIAL ATTACKS

(PRAYERS 181–210)

Foundation Scripture:
"Thou shalt not suffer a witch to live."

– Exodus 22:18

181.
O Lord, let the anointing for divine speed fall on me—what took others 10 years, I will achieve in 1!

Scripture: 1 Kings 18:46

182.
I curse every evil cycle of "almost there but never"—break by fire and Blood of Jesus!

Scripture: Deuteronomy 1:6

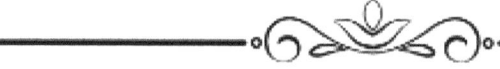

183.
Every spirit of crawling when I should be flying—lose your hold and let me rise like an eagle!

Scripture: Isaiah 40:31

184.

I reject every appointment with stagnation, delay, and shame—divine speed is my portion!

Scripture: Habakkuk 2:3

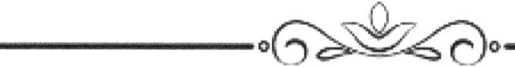

185.

Let every spiritual spider web holding my opportunities be torn apart by the finger of God!

Scripture: Exodus 8:19

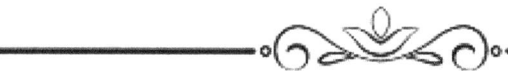

186.

I release fire into every room, vault, or cage where my financial blessings have been stored—open by fire!

Scripture: Isaiah 45:3

187.
Every evil personality sitting on my divine chair of promotion—be unseated by thunder and disgrace!

Scripture: Psalm 75:6-7

188.
I command a divine reversal of every demonic transaction done to divert my wealth and settlement!

Scripture: Proverbs 13:22

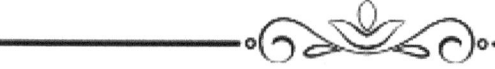

189.
O God arise and break the financial yoke hanging around my neck—I enter prosperity by fire!

Scripture: 3 John 1:2

190.
Every invisible wall resisting my forward march—be blasted by atomic missiles in Jesus' name!

Scripture: Joshua 6:20

191.
I plead the Blood of Jesus over my finances, ideas, and contracts—no more devourers!

Scripture: Philippians 4:19

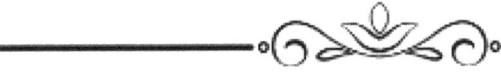

192.
Let divine helpers arise and locate me without delay—I receive the gift of sudden favor!

Scripture: Luke 6:38

193.
I silence every demonic voice speaking "no" when God has already said "yes" over my destiny!

Scripture: Isaiah 14:27

194.
Every curse of financial emptiness—expire now by the Blood of Jesus and fire of the Holy Ghost!

Scripture: Deuteronomy 28:12

195.
I command the resurrection of every dead business, delayed contract, or closed door—come alive by fire!

Scripture: John 11:43-44

196.

O consuming fire, pass through my financial foundation and uproot every embargo placed by witchcraft!

Scripture: Zechariah 1:17-21

197.

Every spiritual hole in my pocket—be sealed now by the Blood of Jesus and divine restoration!

Scripture: Haggai 1:6-7

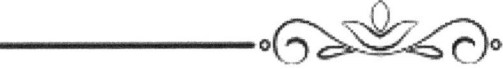

198.

Let divine arrows chase away every demon assigned to scatter my income or delay my harvest!

Scripture: Psalm 35:5-6

199.
I declare prophetic restoration over everything I have lost through delay, failure, and warfare!

Scripture: Joel 2:25

200.
I rise by fire above every limitation—no more delay, no more shame, no more waiting!

Scripture: Isaiah 60:1-2

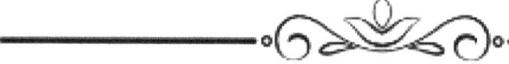

201.
O Lord, catapult me into my season of favor, overflow, and total financial liberty!

Scripture: Deuteronomy 8:18

202.
By divine force, I break out of every prison of joblessness, debt, and empty-handedness!

Scripture: Psalm 126:1

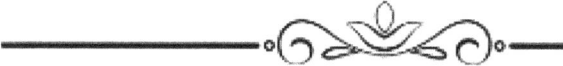

203.
Let every financial curse operating through names, tokens, or covenants—be cancelled by the Blood of Jesus!

Scripture: Numbers 23:20

204.
I declare war against financial dryness—I shall lend to nations and never borrow again!

Scripture: Deuteronomy 28:12

205.

Every household witchcraft power assigned to monitor and frustrate me—receive divine judgment by fire and be buried today!

Scripture: Micah 7:6

206.

I command the thunder of God to locate and scatter every evil gathering of relatives planning my downfall!

Scripture: Psalm 68:1

207.

O Lord, arise and expose every unfriendly friend smiling by day and stabbing by night—let their evil plans backfire!

Scripture: Psalm 35:4-6

208.
I release atomic bomb fire into every evil room, group chat, or shrine where my name is being used—scatter by fire!

Scripture: Psalm 140:11

209.
Any family member turned into a satanic informant—O God, shut their mouths permanently!

Scripture: Psalm 31:18

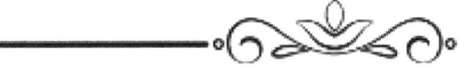

210.
I plead the Blood of Jesus over my relationships—every Judas shall be exposed and disconnected!

Scripture: John 13:27

SECTION EIGHT: MISSILES TO SCATTER HOUSEHOLD WICKEDNESS AND UNFRIENDLY FRIENDS

(PRAYERS 211–240)

Foundation Scripture:

"Thou shalt not suffer a witch to live."

— Exodus 22:18

211.
O consuming fire, enter my father's house and flush out every agent of manipulation and delay!

Scripture: Deuteronomy 23:5

212.
Any wicked elder or bloodline enemy cursing my name—be roasted by the fire of the Lord without remedy!

Scripture: Ezekiel 13:17-18

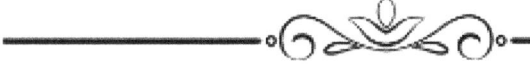

213.
I call on the sword of the Lord to strike every hidden enemy pretending to love me—scatter them in the open!

Scripture: Jeremiah 20:10-11

214.

O Lord, let the light of Your truth expose every deceiver hiding in my inner circle—unmask them by fire!

Scripture: 2 Corinthians 11:14-15

215.

I disconnect my life from every witchcraft covenant initiated by household enemies—break by the Blood of Jesus!

Scripture: Isaiah 28:18

216.

Every unfriendly friend stealing my glory in the spirit—return it now and die by fire!

Scripture: John 10:10

217.

Let the net they have secretly set for me catch their own feet—let them fall into the pit they dug!

Scripture: Psalm 57:6

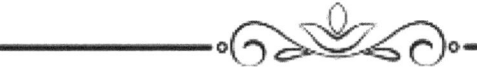

218.

Every power using familiar conversation to gather intel against me—be struck dumb and blind!

Scripture: Acts 13:11

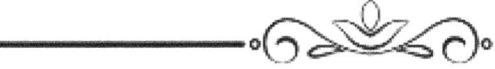

219.

I scatter every witchcraft communication line in my family—no more evil reports shall prosper!

Scripture: Isaiah 8:10

220.
O God of vengeance, strike every household enemy assigned to delay my marriage, breakthrough, or rising!

Scripture: Romans 12:19

221.
I release Holy Ghost missiles into every demonic gathering at night—scatter by thunder, never gather again!

Scripture: Job 5:12-14

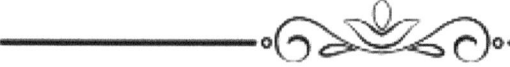

222.
Let every spiritual parasite feeding on my joy, peace, and favor—be roasted without mercy!

Scripture: Obadiah 1:17

223.

Every evil eye in my family monitoring my glory—go blind now in the name of Jesus!

Scripture: 2 Kings 6:18

224.

Let the altar of Jesus Christ speak judgment against any relative sitting on my destiny seat—be unseated and disgraced!

Scripture: Psalm 75:7

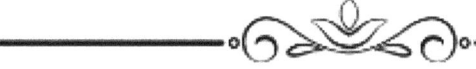

225.

Every ancestral demon delegated by household wickedness to afflict me—be chained forever by the angels of fire!

Scripture: Jude 1:6

226.

O Lord, arise and confuse every dark alliance rising against my calling—scatter them unto desolation!

Scripture: Psalm 33:10

227.

I release fire and thunder against every masquerading spirit hiding in a familiar face—be exposed and destroyed!

Scripture: Matthew 7:15

228.

Every household power that wants me to repeat evil patterns—break now, I am exempted by the Blood of Jesus!

Scripture: Ezekiel 18:2-3

229.

I send Holy Ghost lightning into every compound, room, or shrine where my destiny has been buried—let it be unearthed and restored!

Scripture: Jeremiah 1:10

230.

Every wicked hand secretly manipulating my name— wither now by fire and never rise again!

Scripture: 1 Kings 13:4

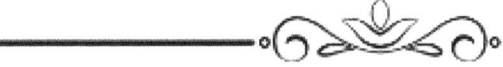

231.

O Jesus, the Lion of Judah, roar into my family and scatter every voice rising against me in secret!

Scripture: Psalm 109:2-3

232.

I release atomic fire into every household charm, spell, or enchantment working against my star—burn now!

Scripture: Galatians 3:13

233.

I declare my total separation from every satanic inheritance, altar, or agreement—by the Blood of Jesus!

Scripture: 2 Corinthians 6:17

234.

Father, release angels of war to surround me night and day—no household arrow shall strike me again!

Scripture: Psalm 91:11-12

235.

O God of restoration, arise and recover everything stolen from me—physically, spiritually, emotionally, and financially!

Scripture: Joel 2:25-26

236.

I release atomic backfire against every witch or wizard that tampered with my destiny—let their arrows return with fire!

Scripture: Psalm 35:8

237.

By the Blood of Jesus, I recover every opportunity, open door, and helper that was manipulated away from me!

Scripture: Isaiah 42:22

238.
Every spiritual warehouse storing my stolen blessings—
open by fire and release my portion!

Scripture: Isaiah 45:3

239.
I command a sevenfold restoration of all my lost glory—
no more delay, no more defeat!

Scripture: Proverbs 6:31

240.
I fire back every curse spoken against my progress—
backfire to sender with multiplied affliction!

Scripture: Numbers 23:23

SECTION NINE: MISSILES FOR DIVINE RESTORATION, DESTINY RECOVERY & BACKFIRE

(PRAYERS 241–260)

Foundation Scripture:
"Thou shalt not suffer a witch to live."

– Exodus 22:18

241.

Every enemy who rejoiced at my loss—O God, arise and shock them with my divine comeback!

Scripture: Micah 7:8

242.

I recover my dream life, my prayer life, my joy, my fire, and my peace by the force of resurrection power!

Scripture: Romans 8:11

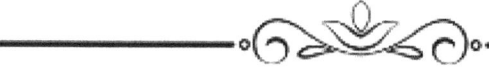

243.

Let the whirlwind of the Lord pursue and dismantle every altar of delay and spiritual robbery!

Scripture: Jeremiah 30:16-17

244.

O Lord, send fire into every evil archive holding my destiny files—let them burn and be released to me!

Scripture: Jeremiah 1:10

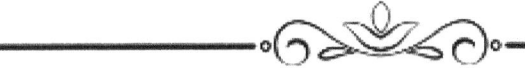

245.

Every spirit of "almost there but never" assigned to keep me in cycles—scatter now by thunder and fire!

Scripture: Isaiah 43:18-19

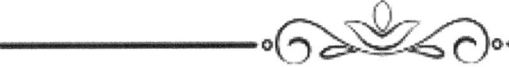

246.

I decree total recovery of my virtues, spiritual gifts, and divine assignments—nothing shall remain missing!

Scripture: 1 Samuel 30:18-19

247.
Let every evil hand that has touched what belongs to me be cut off and disgraced!

Scripture: Zechariah 2:8

248.
Every power that laughed at my failure—watch me rise in power, honor, and divine overflow!

Scripture: Psalm 23:5

249.
I declare supernatural restoration for every loss in relationships, time, money, or inheritance—O God, restore it all!

Scripture: Job 42:10

250.

Every tongue that cursed my destiny, breakthrough, or name—be silenced permanently by fire!

Scripture: Isaiah 54:17

251.

Let the altar of Jehovah speak against every altar where my glory was exchanged—let reversal happen now!

Scripture: Isaiah 61:7

252.

I recover every buried potential, vision, and anointing that was locked up by dark forces—resurrect now!

Scripture: Ezekiel 37:12-14

253.

O God of vengeance, return double trouble to every agent of delay and destiny theft!

Scripture: Nahum 1:2

254.

I declare this day a day of restoration, recovery, and rising—what the enemy stole, I recover all by fire!

Scripture: Obadiah 1:17

255.

Every demonic dream where I was caged, chased, or manipulated—be reversed now by the Blood of Jesus and Holy Ghost fire!

Scripture: Matthew 13:25

256.

O God arise and scatter every spirit of oppression that attacks me in the night—let their assignments catch fire!

Scripture: Psalm 91:5-6

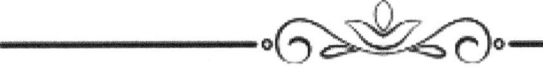

257.

I release atomic bombs into the dream realm—every evil altar, demon, or serpent appearing in my sleep, die by fire!

Scripture: Job 33:14-16

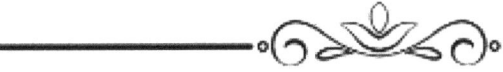

258.

Every evil hand that feeds me in dreams—wither by thunder and catch fire permanently!

Scripture: Matthew 15:13

259.

I withdraw my spirit from every spiritual cage where it has been trapped in the dream world—be loosed by fire!

Scripture: Zechariah 9:11

260.

Every satanic transaction done in my dream to steal my glory—be cancelled by the Blood of Jesus!

Scripture: Colossians 2:14

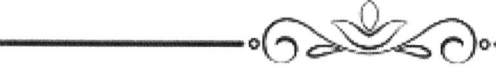

SECTION TEN: MISSILES TO DISMANTLE EVIL DREAMS, SPIRITUAL CAGES & NIGHT ATTACKS

(PRAYERS 261–290)

Foundation Scripture:
"Thou shalt not suffer a witch to live."

– Exodus 22:18

261.

I paralyze every spiritual husband or wife that invades my dreams—be consumed by judgment fire without mercy!

Scripture: Isaiah 54:5

262.

O Lord, let the sword of the Spirit pursue every demon that enters my room at night—let them perish by fire!

Scripture: Ephesians 6:17

263.

I release fire arrows into every marine gate appearing in my dreams—let it collapse with thunder!

Scripture: Psalm 29:7-8

264.

Let the Blood of Jesus wash and seal my pillow, bed, and sleep—no power shall invade my rest again!

Scripture: Psalm 127:2

265.

I cancel every evil implantation done through dreams—vomit it out now by Holy Ghost fire!

Scripture: Mark 16:18

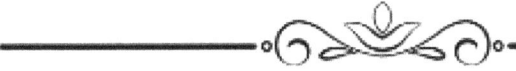

266.

Every satanic animal assigned to chase, bite, or poison me in dreams—die by the fire of God!

Scripture: Luke 10:19

267.
O God of Elijah, arise with fire and destroy every demonic ladder linking my dream life to evil altars!

Scripture: 2 Kings 1:10

268.
I plead the Blood of Jesus over my spiritual eyes—let them be purified to see only what is divine!

Scripture: Matthew 5:8

269.
Every evil dream planted by witches, familiar spirits, or household enemies—catch fire and be erased now!

Scripture: Proverbs 3:24-26

270.
I reclaim every blessing, anointing, or opportunity that was stolen from me in the dream—be restored sevenfold!

Scripture: Joel 2:25

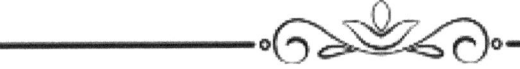

271.
I command every serpent that entered my body through dreams—come out and die by thunder and fire!

Scripture: Acts 28:3-6

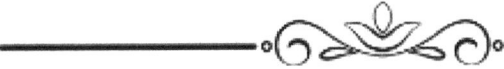

272.
Let every spiritual prison gate be broken down—release my star, virtue, and destiny from bondage!

Scripture: Acts 16:26

273.

O Jesus, Son of David, locate and destroy every spiritual altar that calls my name while I sleep—let it burn now!

Scripture: Psalm 18:6-9

274.

I declare Holy Ghost fire to surround my dream gates—no intruder shall access my mind again!

Scripture: Zechariah 2:5

275.

Every chain of night paralysis and demonic oppression—be broken now by the authority in the name of Jesus!

Scripture: Luke 13:11-13

276.

Let every false prophet or demonic impersonator appearing in my dream be exposed and arrested!

Scripture: 2 Corinthians 11:13-14

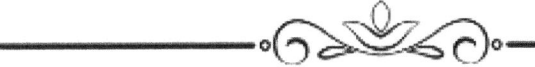

277.

O God, restore my spiritual discernment and dream clarity—I receive the anointing to interpret with fire!

Scripture: Daniel 2:19

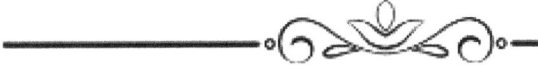

278.

I set Holy Ghost fire around my house, bed, and windows—no witch, wizard, or marine power shall enter again!

Scripture: Isaiah 59:19

279.

I command the thunder of God to strike every satanic dream programmer and dream manipulator assigned to my life!

Scripture: Jeremiah 23:29

280.

Let every python spirit wrapping me in the spirit realm be cut to pieces by the sword of the Lord!

Scripture: Isaiah 27:1

281.

I declare freedom from every sexual covenant, soul tie, or exchange made through dreams—break now in Jesus' name!

Scripture: Matthew 19:6

282.
Let every witchcraft gathering planning dream attacks—scatter without mercy, never to regroup again!

Scripture: Psalm 118:12

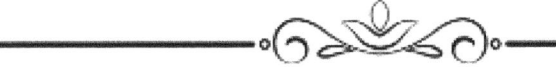

283.
I seal my dream life with the Blood of Jesus—no darkness shall infiltrate my rest again!

Scripture: Revelation 12:11

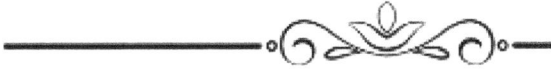

284.
O Lord, fill my dream life with fire, revelation, and divine encounters—no more fear, confusion, or delay!

Scripture: Job 33:15-16

285.
Every covenant formed through sex in the dream—be broken now by the Blood of Jesus and consumed by fire!

Scripture: Isaiah 28:18

286.
I command every spirit spouse visiting me in the dream—be arrested by the fire of the Holy Ghost and chained forever!

Scripture: 1 Corinthians 6:15-16

287.
Any food I ate in the dream to initiate sickness, delay, or bondage—be vomited now by fire!

Scripture: Mark 16:18

288.
O Lord, deliver me from every serpent chasing or biting me in the dream—let the serpent die instantly by thunder!

Scripture: Luke 10:19

289.
Every dream where dogs chased, bit, or licked me—be cancelled by the Blood of Jesus! Let the source dry up by fire!

Scripture: Psalm 22:16

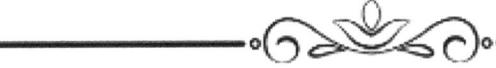

290.
I scatter every demonic bird that appeared in my dream—let them fall down and burn by divine lightning!

Scripture: Isaiah 31:5

SECTION ELEVEN: MISSILES TO DESTROY EVIL DREAM ENCOUNTERS, SICKNESS YOKES & DEMONIC BODILY MANIPULATIONS

(PRAYERS 291–320)

Foundation Scripture:
"Thou shalt not suffer a witch to live."

— Exodus 22:18

291.

Every power using my body to fly, fight, or perform rituals in the dream—be disconnected and disgraced by the Blood!

Scripture: Isaiah 8:18

292.

I disconnect from every occult gathering, meeting, or circle I found myself in during dreams—let that altar scatter now!

Scripture: 2 Corinthians 6:14-17

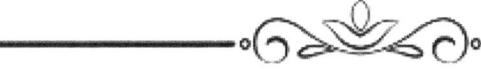

293.

Every covenant of darkness enforced through demonic symbols in dreams—be broken by the Blood of the Everlasting Covenant!

Scripture: Hebrews 13:20

294.

I release Holy Ghost fire to burn every altar I was summoned to in the dream—let it turn to ashes!

Scripture: Deuteronomy 7:5

295.

Any power using my dream life to renew sickness or bondage—be terminated now without mercy!

Scripture: Psalm 6:2

296.

I declare: I shall no longer be used as a witchcraft instrument in any dream realm—my soul is redeemed!

Scripture: Psalm 124:7

297.
O God of Elijah, consume every spiritual trap laid in my dream path—let the setter fall into their own net!

Scripture: Psalm 141:10

298.
I anoint my body and mind with the Blood of Jesus—no demon shall enter my vessel again through dreams!

Scripture: 1 Thessalonians 5:23

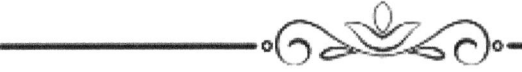

299.
I cast out every evil spirit deposited in me through dream encounters—get out by fire in Jesus' name!

Scripture: Matthew 10:1

300.
Let every token, mark, or spiritual garment placed on me in a dream—be consumed by Holy Ghost fire!

Scripture: Zechariah 3:4

301.
I renounce every satanic assignment I was given in a dream—let it expire and return to sender by fire!

Scripture: Psalm 35:4-6

302.
Every counterfeit version of me used by the enemy in dreams—be destroyed now in Jesus' mighty name!

Scripture: Isaiah 54:17

303.

I command every manipulation against my health through night encounters—die now and leave no trace!

Scripture: Jeremiah 30:17

304.

Let every witchcraft veil covering my dream vision be torn to pieces—I receive clarity and divine revelation!

Scripture: Daniel 2:22

305.

I cancel every dream of backwardness, falling, or failing—reverse by fire, I move forward in power!

Scripture: Philippians 3:13

306.

O Lord, purge my dream life with fire—let no impure seed find rest in my subconscious!

Scripture: Malachi 3:3

307.

I disconnect my bloodline from generational dream manipulators—no more inherited dream attacks!

Scripture: Galatians 3:13

308.

Let every agent who appears in my dream to seduce, steal, or confuse—be permanently silenced by thunder!

Scripture: Proverbs 6:12-15

309.
Every dream of dying, funerals, or burial grounds—I cancel you now by the Blood of Jesus!

Scripture: Psalm 118:17

310.
I declare war against every dream of poverty, shame, and destruction—scatter by Holy Ghost fire!

Scripture: 2 Kings 6:17

311.
Let every symbol of defeat, chains, or cages in my dream—be destroyed and replaced with crowns of victory!

Scripture: Revelation 3:11

312.

O God arise, and speak to me clearly through my dreams—let my dream life become a prophetic altar!

Scripture: Job 33:15-16

313.

I command my sleep and dream realm to be holy, sanctified, and reserved for divine encounters only!

Scripture: Acts 2:17

314.

I decree: I am delivered, my soul is rescued, my body is healed, and my dreams are fire-guarded—IN JESUS' NAME!

Scripture: Obadiah 1:17

315.

O Lord my Healer, arise and let every root of infirmity in my body be uprooted and consumed by Holy Ghost fire!

Scripture: Jeremiah 30:17

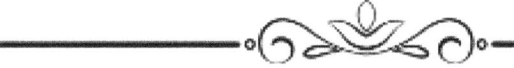

316.

Every inherited sickness, genetic affliction, or bloodline disease—dry up now by the Blood of Jesus!

Scripture: Isaiah 53:5

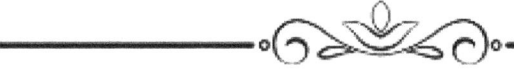

317.

I command every arrow of sickness fired into my body to backfire sevenfold in Jesus' name!

Scripture: Psalm 91:5-6

318.

By the stripes of Jesus Christ, I declare total healing over my bones, organs, blood, and immune system!

Scripture: 1 Peter 2:24

319.

Any altar of infirmity raised against my life—scatter now by fire and thunder!

Scripture: Psalm 107:20

320

Let every hidden serpent of affliction in my body be exposed, uprooted, and burned to ashes!

Scripture: Acts 28:5

SECTION TWELVE: MISSILES FOR HEALING, LONG LIFE & DELIVERANCE FROM INCURABLE SICKNESSES (PRAYERS 321–350)

Foundation Scripture:
"Thou shalt not suffer a witch to live."

– Exodus 22:18

321.

I break every covenant of premature death and declare: I shall not die but live to declare the works of the Lord!

Scripture: Psalm 118:17

322.

O God of vengeance, let every sickness sponsored by witchcraft return to sender with multiplied affliction!

Scripture: Deuteronomy 28:7

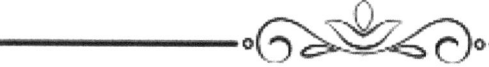

323.

Let divine healing rivers flow through my body—cleansing every toxin, pain, and demonic seed!

Scripture: Ezekiel 47:9

324.

I reject every death sentence spoken over my life—let it be cancelled by the Blood of the Lamb!

Scripture: Colossians 2:14

325.

Every voice saying "this sickness is incurable"—I silence you by the resurrection power of Jesus Christ!

Scripture: Luke 1:37

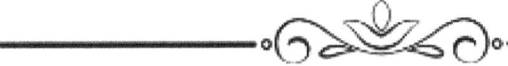

326.

I declare: I am healed from every known and unknown affliction—this is my covenant right in Christ!

Scripture: Exodus 15:26

327.
O Lord, replace every dying organ, tissue, or blood cell with new divine parts from Heaven's storehouse!

Scripture: Psalm 103:3-5

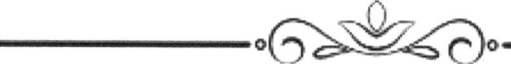

328.
Let every spirit of paralysis, stroke, weakness, and terminal disease be judged and cast out by fire!

Scripture: Luke 13:11-13

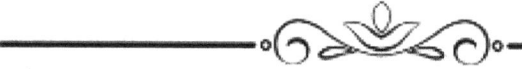

329.
I plead the Blood of Jesus over my brain, heart, lungs, kidneys, and every system—no malfunction shall continue!

Scripture: Isaiah 38:5

330.
Every attack on my mental health—be reversed now by the power in the name of Jesus!

Scripture: 2 Timothy 1:7

331.
Every arrow of cancer, diabetes, or autoimmune disorder—jump out now and die by fire!

Scripture: Matthew 15:13

332.
O Lord, restore the years I've lost to sickness, medication, and limitation—bring me into full restoration!

Scripture: Joel 2:25

333.
Every evil monitoring spirit behind my sickness—go blind and burn to ashes now!

Scripture: Psalm 27:2

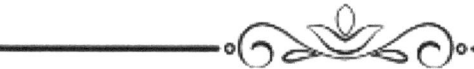

334.
I renounce every negative report and diagnosis contrary to God's promise—whose report shall I believe? I believe the Lord!

Scripture: Isaiah 53:1

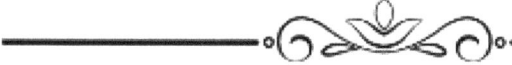

335.
O Breath of God, breathe new life into my body—I receive strength, vitality, and divine longevity!

Scripture: Genesis 2:7

336.
I command spiritual infection, affliction, and pollution—dry up now from my system without trace!

Scripture: Malachi 4:2

337.
Every power waiting for my obituary—wait in vain! I shall live long and finish my divine assignment!

Scripture: Psalm 91:16

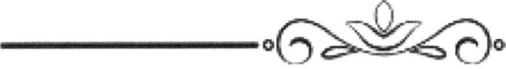

338.
Let the Blood of Jesus purge my bloodline of every generational infirmity and hereditary torment!

Scripture: Galatians 3:13

339.
I break the pattern of repeated hospital admissions, emergency attacks, and lingering sickness—scatter now!

Scripture: Nahum 1:9

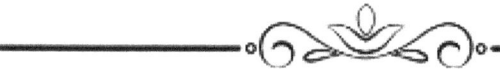

340.
Let fire descend upon every altar of infirmity in my father's or mother's house—be destroyed without remedy!

Scripture: Judges 6:25

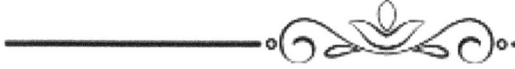

341.
I arise as a firebrand of healing—I shall lay hands on the sick, and they shall recover!

Scripture: Mark 16:17-18

342.

O Jehovah Rapha, cover me with Your healing mantle—let sickness vanish and health overflow!

Scripture: Exodus 15:26

343.

Every satanic exchange that transferred affliction to me— be reversed by the Blood of Jesus now!

Scripture: Isaiah 61:3

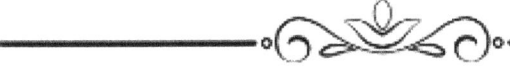

344.

I declare boldly: I am healed, I am whole, I am strong, and I shall fulfill my years in divine health—IN JESUS' NAME!

Scripture: 3 John 1:2

345.
Every evil pattern of rising and falling in my life—break and scatter now by the Blood of Jesus!

Scripture: Psalm 34:19

346.
I cancel every recurring cycle of delay, disappointment, and rejection—be terminated permanently!

Scripture: Nahum 1:9

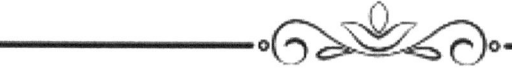

347.
O Lord, deliver me from inherited patterns of poverty, marital delay, and untimely death!

Scripture: Galatians 3:13

348.
I command every evil calendar marking seasons of failure in my life—catch fire and burn to ashes!

Scripture: Isaiah 10:27

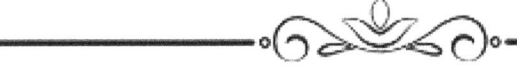

349.
I break the chain of "almost there but never"—I enter into complete manifestation by fire!

Scripture: Philippians 1:6

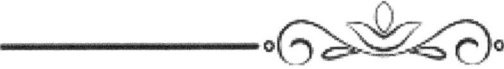

350.
Every evil cycle repeating itself in my bloodline—I escape by the Blood of Jesus and break free forever!

Scripture: Romans 8:2

SECTION THIRTEEN: MISSILES TO BREAK EVIL PATTERNS AND CYCLES (PRAYERS 351–380)

Foundation Scripture:
"Thou shalt not suffer a witch to live."

— Exodus 22:18

351.
I declare war against backwardness and spiritual retrogression—move forward by fire!

Scripture: Exodus 14:15

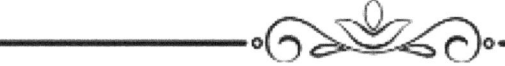

352.
Every foundational curse causing generational failure—expire now by the power of Jehovah!

Scripture: Numbers 23:23

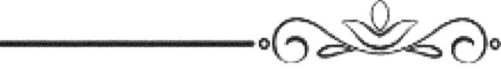

353.
I break the yoke of stagnation that has followed me from childhood—be shattered without repair!

Scripture: Psalm 40:2

354.

Every hidden altar enforcing evil family patterns—collapse now under divine judgment!

Scripture: Judges 6:25

355.

I renounce the covenant of shame and repeated disgrace—I shall not suffer like my forefathers!

Scripture: Isaiah 61:7

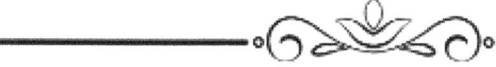

356.

Every spiritual limitation tied to my surname or clan—be cut off by the sword of the Lord!

Scripture: Matthew 10:36

357.
O Lord, disconnect me from patterns of infirmity that rise at the edge of breakthrough!

Scripture: Psalm 107:20

358.
Every repetitive struggle in marriage, finance, or ministry—break and scatter by fire!

Scripture: Isaiah 54:17

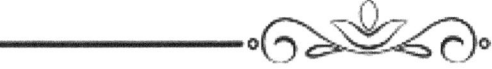

359.
I reject the spirit of delay that rises yearly at specific times—I cancel every demonic cycle!

Scripture: Psalm 31:15

360.

Let the power of divine exemption rest upon me—I am not a candidate for generational affliction!

Scripture: Exodus 12:13

361.

I declare my escape from inherited failure—I shall succeed where others fell!

Scripture: Romans 8:37

362.

Every pattern of late marriage or barrenness in my bloodline—be reversed now by the Blood of Jesus!

Scripture: Exodus 23:26

363.
O God arise, disconnect me from circles of betrayal, loss, and false promises—deliver me by fire!

Scripture: Psalm 124:7

364.
I break every agreement with the pattern of oppression and setback—I walk in liberty by fire!

Scripture: John 8:36

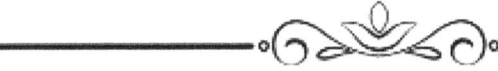

365.
Every spiritual embargo preventing new things—be lifted now, let the floodgates open!

Scripture: Isaiah 43:19

366.

I reject every chain of witchcraft programming repeating battles into my seasons—scatter now!

Scripture: Micah 2:13

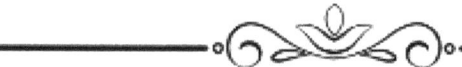

367.

Let every demonic gatekeeper enforcing cycles of loss and delay—be unseated by fire and thunder!

Scripture: Psalm 24:7

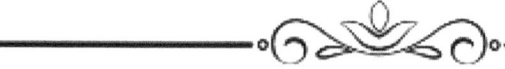

368.

I break the curse of untimely failure that rises after major success—be consumed without mercy!

Scripture: Job 22:28

369.
I refuse to follow the footsteps of failure—I choose the path of fire, favor, and fulfillment!

Scripture: Psalm 16:11

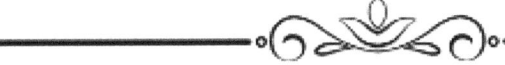

370.
O Lord, rewrite my story—I shall not repeat the errors of my ancestors!

Scripture: 2 Corinthians 5:17

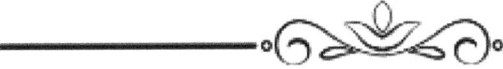

371.
Every spiritual chain holding my bloodline to altars of affliction—break now in Jesus' name!

Scripture: Zechariah 9:11-12

372.

I invoke divine restoration and acceleration—every wasted year shall be redeemed now!

Scripture: Joel 2:25

373.

I declare: I am a curse breaker, a pattern destroyer, and a testimony carrier. I walk in generational fire!

Scripture: Obadiah 1:17

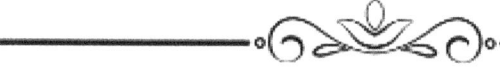

374.

O Lord, by Your power, I possess every door of breakthrough that has been shut against me—open by fire!

Scripture: Revelation 3:8

375.
I command every satanic padlock, chain, and gate blocking my progress—break now by thunder and the Blood of Jesus!

Scripture: Isaiah 22:22

376.
Every evil strongman guarding my destiny gates—be arrested and overthrown now in the name of Jesus!

Scripture: Matthew 12:29

377.
I receive divine keys to unlock every door of financial, marital, and ministerial breakthrough prepared for me!

Scripture: Matthew 16:19

378.

O Lord, release angelic reinforcements to bulldoze every spiritual barrier in my path—let my access be undeniable!

Scripture: Psalm 103:20

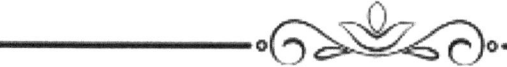

379.

Let the wind of the Spirit carry me into open doors of favor, elevation, and influence—no delay, no resistance!

Scripture: Zechariah 4:6-7

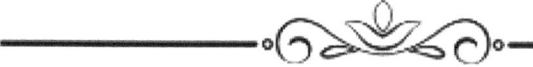

380.

Every demonic traffic controlling spirit causing spiritual delays—clear out by fire in Jesus' name!

Scripture: Exodus 14:14

SECTION FOURTEEN: MISSILES TO POSSESS OPEN DOORS, DIVINE SPEED & NEW BEGINNINGS (PRAYERS 381–410)

Foundation Scripture:
"Thou shalt not suffer a witch to live."

– Exodus 22:18

381.

I declare divine acceleration—what took others years, I shall recover in months by Holy Ghost speed!

Scripture: 1 Kings 18:46

382.

O God of new beginnings, reset my life and destiny into divine order—restore what the enemy disrupted!

Scripture: Isaiah 43:18-19

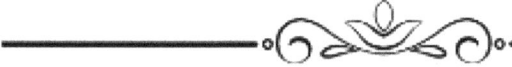

383.

I reject stagnation and delay—I move forward by grace, by fire, and by prophecy!

Scripture: Deuteronomy 1:6-7

384.
Every demonic voice saying "not yet" over my open door—
be silenced forever by the Blood of the Lamb!

Scripture: Numbers 23:20

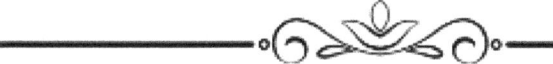

385.
I decree: new chapters, new levels, new favor, and new
fire begin for me today!

Scripture: Lamentations 3:22-23

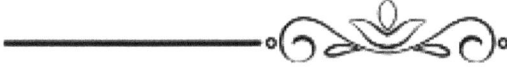

386.
Let divine speed replace every delay I have suffered in past
seasons—recover all now!

Scripture: Joel 2:25-26

387.
O God, lift me out of obscurity and plant me in the field of visibility—let my light break forth!

Scripture: Matthew 5:14-16

388.
I unlock new territories, fresh opportunities, and global connections by fire and faith!

Scripture: Genesis 13:17

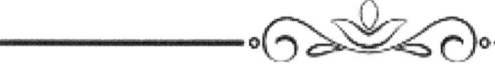

389.
I reject every evil delay tactic—angelic traffic, spiritual detours, and diversion spirits, be removed!

Scripture: Acts 12:10

390.
Let the anointing for "next-level breakthrough" rest upon me now—I am moving forward, not backward!

Scripture: Philippians 3:13-14

391.
I prophesy divine surprises, unexpected favor, and sudden answers into my atmosphere—explode now!

Scripture: Ephesians 3:20

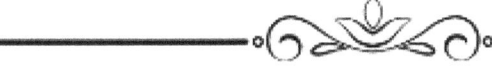

392.
Every old door that must close for my new season to open—close permanently by divine instruction!

Scripture: Ecclesiastes 3:1

393.

O Lord, let the next 12 months of my life be filled with divine speed, open doors, and established prophecy!

Scripture: Amos 9:13

394.

I possess the gates of my enemies and take over every territory promised to my bloodline!

Scripture: Genesis 22:17

395.

Father, close every counterfeit door meant to delay or destroy me—let only Your doors remain open!

Scripture: Proverbs 14:12

396.
Let divine fire go ahead of me and clear the way—no obstacle shall stop me this time!

Scripture: Deuteronomy 31:8

397.
I decree divine relocation to the place of fulfillment—no more wasted efforts in dead places!

Scripture: Genesis 12:1-2

398.
O Lord, breathe on my dreams, plans, and pursuits—let new life rise again by resurrection power!

Scripture: Romans 8:11

399.
I enter the divine realm of "more than enough"—no lack, no delay, no struggle, no sorrow!

Scripture: Psalm 23:1

400.
Every "almost there" testimony—manifest now! I will not miss my season again!

Scripture: Habakkuk 2:3

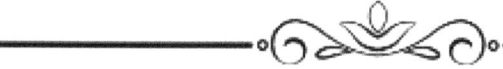

401.
I declare open doors over my family, ministry, business, and destiny—no witch or altar shall shut it!

Scripture: Revelation 3:7-8

402.

I walk into divine appointments, covenant connections, and new beginnings by the fire of the Holy Ghost—IN JESUS' NAME!

Scripture: Psalm 102:13

403

Every voice of accusation speaking from altars, covens, or bloodlines—be silenced by the Blood of Jesus!

Scripture: Revelation 12:11

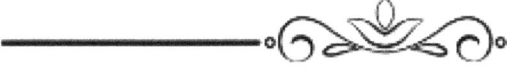

404.

O Lord, arise and turn every satanic verdict issued against me into ashes—let divine mercy override evil judgment!

Scripture: Romans 8:33-34

405.
I cancel every demonic prophecy spoken against my future—I believe the report of the Lord!

Scripture: Isaiah 53:1

406.
Let the thunder of God scatter every evil speaker calling my name for destruction in the spirit realm!

Scripture: Psalm 29:3-5

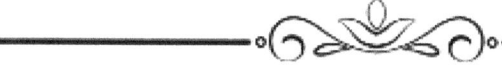

407.
I blot out every satanic handwriting, covenant, or report against my name by the Blood of Jesus!

Scripture: Colossians 2:14

408.
Every voice from my past speaking limitation into my present—be shut down by the mercy of God!

Scripture: Lamentations 3:22-23

409.
I silence every voice of fear, failure, sickness, and rejection—only the voice of victory shall remain!

Scripture: 2 Timothy 1:7

410.
Every monitoring spirit spreading evil reports about me—go blind and be silenced forever!

Scripture: 2 Kings 6:18

SECTION FIFTEEN: MISSILES TO SILENCE EVIL VOICES, ACCUSATIONS & DEMONIC REPORTS

(PRAYERS 411–440)

Foundation Scripture:
"Thou shalt not suffer a witch to live."

— Exodus 22:18

411.

O Lord, let every witchcraft voice that rises at midnight to report me be silenced permanently by thunder!

Scripture: Psalm 35:4-6

412.

Every false witness assigned to damage my name—be exposed and disgraced by the fire of God!

Scripture: Proverbs 19:5

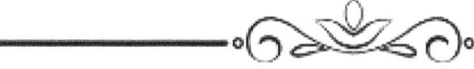

413.

I speak confusion into the camp of every demonic reporter—scatter without recovery!

Scripture: Psalm 68:1

414.

Let the voice of the Blood of Jesus speak louder than the voice of generational curses in my family!

Scripture: Hebrews 12:24

415.

I shut down every evil ancestral voice declaring repeated failure in my life—be silenced by fire!

Scripture: Ezekiel 18:2-4

416.

I revoke every word curse spoken over my destiny—let it break and reverse by the Blood of the Covenant!

Scripture: Galatians 3:13

417.
O God arise and let every demonic mocker around me be silenced by the sound of my breakthrough!

Scripture: Psalm 23:5

418.
Let every voice from the grave summoning my name—be silenced and buried forever!

Scripture: Isaiah 28:18

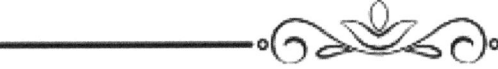

419.
Every satanic voice in my dreams planting fear and bondage—be muted by the voice of Jehovah!

Scripture: Job 33:15-16

420.

I silence every voice of death, delay, and failure echoing in my ears—let them vanish now!

Scripture: Psalm 118:17

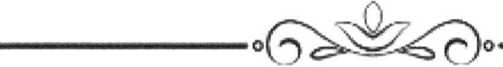

421.

Let the trumpet of divine mercy drown every accusation laid before satanic courts!

Scripture: Romans 8:1

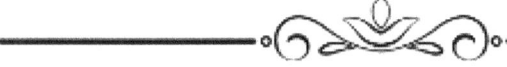

422.

I reject and reverse every evil announcement made in the spirit realm concerning my family—let it burn now!

Scripture: Psalm 94:23

423.

Every demonic reporter whispering lies into the ears of my destiny helpers—be silenced now by Holy Ghost fire!

Scripture: Isaiah 54:17

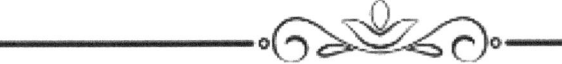

424.

I command every demonic speaker in the second heaven assigned to block my prayers—shut up and fall down!

Scripture: Daniel 10:12-13

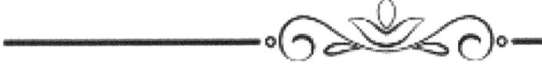

425.

Let the voice of the Lion of Judah roar over every opposing altar trying to silence my progress!

Scripture: Revelation 5:5

426.
I renounce every evil word spoken in anger, bitterness, jealousy, or witchcraft—be broken now!

Scripture: Numbers 23:23

427.
I cancel every secret declaration against my calling, business, and home—scatter by thunder!

Scripture: Psalm 140:11

428.
Every voice of envy, hatred, or evil monitoring rising against me—be silenced permanently!

Scripture: Psalm 64:2-8

429.
I declare that only the Word of God shall stand in my life—every contrary word, be reversed!

Scripture: Isaiah 46:10

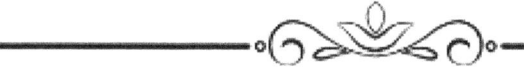

430.
Let the roar of the Holy Spirit silence every witch, warlock, and occult voice invoking my name!

Scripture: Isaiah 59:19

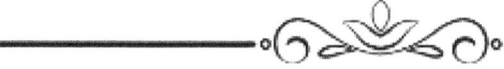

431.
I receive the voice of favor, breakthrough, and divine remembrance—let it echo louder than accusations!

Scripture: Esther 6:1-3

432.

I decree: no voice shall rise again against me—only the voice of God shall lead me forward!

Scripture: Psalm 29:4

433.

O Lord of Hosts, arise and scatter every global and local network of witchcraft assigned against my life—scatter by thunder!

Scripture: Psalm 68:1

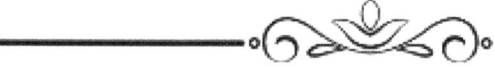

434.

I release the judgment fire of God against every coven meeting this night against my family—let them be consumed!

Scripture: Isaiah 66:15-16

435.
Every satanic priest invoking my name or picture on an altar—be roasted without remedy by Holy Ghost fire!

Scripture: 1 Kings 18:36-40

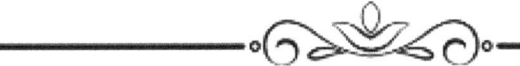

436.
I command every witchcraft roundtable where my case is being discussed—explode by the fury of God!

Scripture: Psalm 94:23

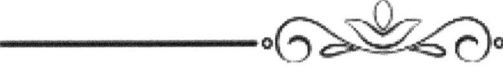

437.
Let every marine, forest, desert, or sky altar working together against me—break apart and scatter now!

Scripture: Deuteronomy 12:3

438.

I release confusion and fire into the heart of every witch, warlock, and occultist assigned to monitor me!

Scripture: 2 Chronicles 20:22-24

439.

I revoke every incantation, spell, or blood sacrifice made against me—let the Blood of Jesus speak louder!

Scripture: Hebrews 12:24

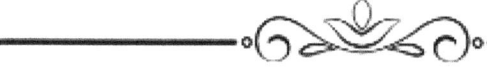

440.

Let the judgment thunder of Jehovah strike every witchcraft conference plotting my death—scatter unto desolation!

Scripture: Psalm 29:7-9

SECTION SIXTEEN: MISSILES FOR JUDGMENT AGAINST WITCHCRAFT NETWORKS, COVENS & OCCULT ALTARS

(PRAYERS 441–470)

Foundation Scripture:

"Thou shalt not suffer a witch to live."

— Exodus 22:18

441.

I break the covenant of unity among witches targeting my glory—let confusion divide them now!

Scripture: Genesis 11:6-8

442.

Every altar where they burn incense or sacrifice against my calling—receive the fury of God and be shattered!

Scripture: Leviticus 20:27

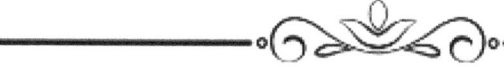

443.

I command Holy Ghost bombs to detonate inside every dark stronghold where my name is hidden—scatter now!

Scripture: Jeremiah 23:29

444.

Let every demonic network linking diviners, false prophets, and witches against me—be destroyed by the sword of God!

Scripture: Ezekiel 13:18-21

445.

O Lord, arrest every demonic courier carrying evil messages on my behalf—bind them in chains of fire!

Scripture: Nahum 1:6

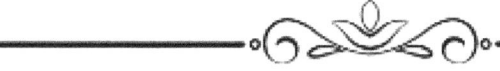

446.

I release Holy Ghost acid into every cauldron, bowl, or pot used to manipulate my image—let it melt and backfire!

Scripture: Ezekiel 11:11

447.
Let every witchcraft mirror projecting my life be broken by the hammer of God—scatter irreversibly!

Scripture: Jeremiah 23:29

448.
I silence every mouth chanting my name in incantations and demonic recitations—let their tongues cleave!

Scripture: Psalm 31:17-18

449.
Every occult agreement made to delay, defile, or destroy my future—scatter by thunder and be reversed by fire!

Scripture: Job 5:12-14

450.
O God of Elijah, answer by fire and devour every enchantment programmed against my destiny!

Scripture: 2 Kings 1:10

451.
Let every witch that refuses to repent be exposed, disgraced, and judged publicly in Jesus' name!

Scripture: Psalm 35:1-8

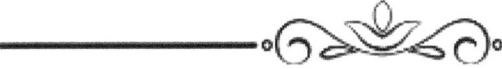

452.
I pour the Blood of Jesus upon every demonic registry, book, or scroll bearing my name—let it be wiped out now!

Scripture: Colossians 2:14

453.

I declare divine judgment upon every sponsor of witchcraft attacks against my health, family, or finances—be visited by God!

Scripture: Psalm 7:15-16

454.

Let fire fall upon every spiritual weapon formed against me—burn to ashes and scatter by thunder!

Scripture: Isaiah 54:17

455.

Every voice of satanic intercessors crying out for my destruction—be silenced by divine vengeance!

Scripture: Lamentations 3:60-66

456.
I send the whirlwind of fire into every underground, forest, or marine base where witches operate against my glory—scatter now!

Scripture: Psalm 18:13-14

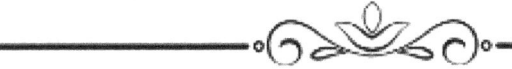

457.
Let every satanic surveillance system tracking my family be electrocuted by the lightning of Jehovah!

Scripture: Job 36:32-33

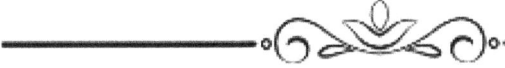

458.
I command supernatural fire to consume every symbol, totem, or effigy representing me in demonic places!

Scripture: Deuteronomy 7:25

459.
Every global altar networked against my breakthrough—scatter into seven pieces now in the name of Jesus!

Scripture: Deuteronomy 28:7

460.
Let God arise and strike terror into every occult camp assigned to resist my next level—scatter and die!

Scripture: Psalm 144:6

461.
I call for divine thunder and whirlwind to judge and destroy every anti-Christ altar in my territory!

Scripture: Jeremiah 30:23

462.

I decree: every altar, every witch, every network—be destroyed without remedy, and let the fire of Jehovah reign forever!

Scripture: Obadiah 1:18

463.

Every seed of witchcraft unknowingly planted in my bloodline—be uprooted by the fire of God now!

Scripture: Matthew 15:13

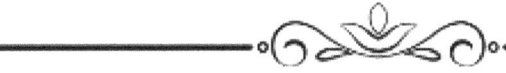

464.

I plead the Blood of Jesus over my children—no evil altar shall speak into their lives!

Scripture: Isaiah 54:13

465.

I break every generational curse targeting my children and descendants—be destroyed by the Blood of the Everlasting Covenant!

Scripture: Galatians 3:13

466

Every witchcraft initiation done through names, birth rituals, or family altars—be reversed now by thunder and fire!

Scripture: Jeremiah 1:10

467.

I disconnect my children from every satanic inheritance, covenant, or spiritual chain!

Scripture: Ezekiel 18:2-3

468.
O God arise and deliver my children from every foundational bondage passed down through bloodlines!

Scripture: Psalm 112:2

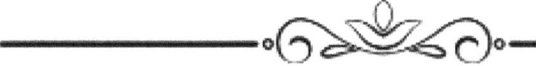

469.
I declare my seed shall be mighty in the land—no spirit of darkness shall possess their destiny!

Scripture: Psalm 127:3-5

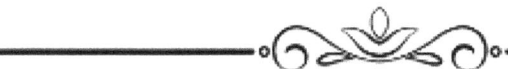

470.
Every monitoring spirit assigned to watch my children—be blinded and banished forever by Holy Ghost fire!

Scripture: 2 Kings 6:17-18

SECTION SEVENTEEN: MISSILES TO UPROOT WITCHCRAFT SEEDS IN CHILDREN, BLOODLINES & FUTURE GENERATIONS (PRAYERS 471–500)

Foundation Scripture:
"Thou shalt not suffer a witch to live."

— Exodus 22:18

471.

I cancel every evil pattern programmed to repeat itself through my lineage—this chain breaks now!

Scripture: Isaiah 10:27

472.

Every evil pronouncement spoken over my children in anger, envy, or witchcraft—be reversed by the Blood of Jesus!

Scripture: Numbers 23:8

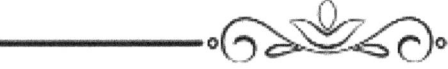

473.

Let every demonic dream or nightmare attacking my children's sleep be terminated now by angelic intervention!

Scripture: Psalm 91:11

474.

I anoint the heads, hands, and feet of my children—they shall walk in favor, purity, and power!

Scripture: Exodus 29:7

475.

Every hidden enemy befriending my children to sow witchcraft seeds—be exposed and scattered!

Scripture: Psalm 55:12-15

476.

Let the spirit of discernment rest upon my children—they shall not be deceived or manipulated!

Scripture: Proverbs 3:5-6

477.
I release prophetic intercession over my bloodline—we shall serve the Lord in purity and fire!

Scripture: Joshua 24:15

478.
Every altar calling the names of my children for bondage—be swallowed by the Blood of Jesus!

Scripture: Revelation 12:11

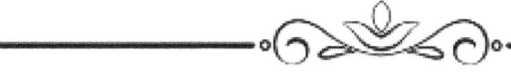

479.
I break the hold of ancestral spirits attempting to claim ownership over my seed—release them now by thunder!

Scripture: Colossians 2:15

480.

O Lord, visit the foundation of my children—rebuild them in righteousness and holiness!

Scripture: Isaiah 54:14

481.

I declare war against every generational affliction trying to rise in my bloodline—scatter now in Jesus' name!

Scripture: Obadiah 1:17

482.

My children shall not be used by witches, altars, or demons—they are fire-branded and Holy Spirit-filled!

Scripture: Joel 2:28

483.
Every demonic expectation set for my children—be disappointed and reversed by the Blood of the Lamb!

Scripture: Job 5:12

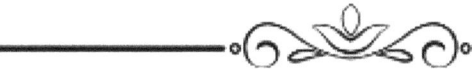

484.
I cover my descendants with Holy Ghost fire—they will not follow evil paths or ancestral rebellion!

Scripture: Deuteronomy 30:19

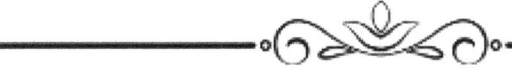

485.
I seal the destiny of every child connected to me with the Blood of Jesus—no power shall corrupt them!

Scripture: Hebrews 13:20-21

486.

Let every evil covenant made on behalf of my children— be cancelled now by divine intervention!

Scripture: Isaiah 28:18

487.

O Lord, assign warring angels to protect the future of my household from demonic ambush!

Scripture: Psalm 91:11-12

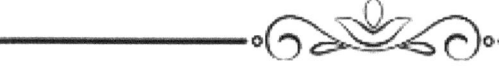

488.

I declare: My children and grandchildren shall walk in divine wisdom, prophetic fire, and kingdom assignment!

Scripture: Proverbs 4:7

489.

Every marine, serpentine, or ancestral spirit seeking to claim my seed—be bound in chains and cast into outer darkness!

Scripture: Jude 1:6

490.

I decree prophetic separation between my lineage and every evil tree planted by forefathers—let it be uprooted by fire!

Scripture: Matthew 3:10

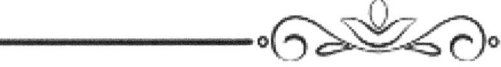

491.

O Lord, fill every child in my household with Your Spirit from a young age—they shall walk in truth and purity!

Scripture: 1 Samuel 2:26

492.

I declare total deliverance, prophetic activation, and fire preservation over every child born and unborn connected to me—IN JESUS' NAME!

Scripture: Psalm 71:5-6

493.

Every spiritual husband or wife assigned to torment my life—be arrested and judged by the fire of the Holy Ghost!

Scripture: Isaiah 54:5

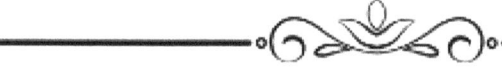

494.

I break every covenant of spiritual marriage entered knowingly or unknowingly—be revoked by the Blood of Jesus!

Scripture: Isaiah 28:18

495.

I renounce every satanic soul tie created through ungodly relationships—be cut off by the sword of the Lord!

Scripture: 2 Corinthians 6:14-17

496.

Every spirit spouse assigned to defile my dreams, delay my marriage, or hinder my destiny—be bound in chains of darkness forever!

Scripture: Jude 1:6

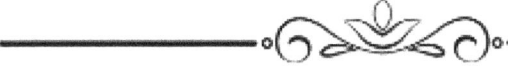

497.

I command the fire of God to consume every ring, chain, or spiritual token used to bind me to a spirit spouse!

Scripture: Acts 19:19

498.

I reverse every spiritual exchange of glory, favor, or health performed through spiritual marriage—be undone now!

Scripture: Psalm 124:7

499.

O Lord, restore my physical, emotional, and spiritual wholeness—I disconnect from every demonic intimacy!

Scripture: 1 Corinthians 6:19-20

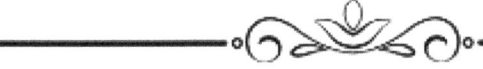

500.

Let every altar that enforces spiritual marriage against my life catch fire and scatter to ashes!

Scripture: Judges 6:25

CONFRONT SPIRITUAL MARRIAGES, SOUL TIES & EMOTIONAL BONDAGE (PRAYERS 501–530)

Foundation Scripture:
"Thou shalt not suffer a witch to live."

— Exodus 22:18

501.

I break free from every invisible chain of emotional torment, obsession, or manipulation—let peace be restored!

Scripture: John 14:27

502.

I recover my virtue, my honor, and my freedom from every evil covenant formed through intimacy or sexual sin!

Scripture: Joel 2:25

503.

Every delay in my earthly marriage caused by spirit spouses—expire now by thunder and fire!

Scripture: Genesis 2:18

504.
I shut every spiritual gateway through which spirit spouses gain access to my dreams—be sealed by the Blood of Jesus!

Scripture: Isaiah 22:22

505.
I command every spiritual baby, child, or responsibility assigned to bind me to the spirit world—be nullified by fire!

Scripture: Galatians 5:1

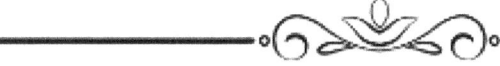

506.
Every deposit from spirit spouses—fire of God, flush it out of my body, soul, and spirit!

Scripture: Ezekiel 36:25

507.

I disconnect from every seductive power of Jezebel, Delilah, or marine spirits—my soul belongs to Jesus Christ!

Scripture: Revelation 2:20

508.

Every satanic veil covering my marital favor—catch fire and be removed now!

Scripture: Isaiah 25:7

509.

I call forth my God-ordained spouse—let the delay end and divine connection be released!

Scripture: Proverbs 18:22

510.

I command every monitoring agent sent by spirit spouses—go blind and perish by thunder!

Scripture: Psalm 35:5-6

511.

I break the spirit of loneliness, rejection, and emotional instability—Holy Spirit, restore me in full!

Scripture: Isaiah 61:1-3

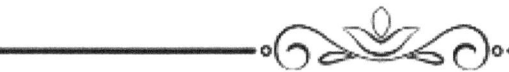

512.

Let the sword of Jehovah cut off every ancient chain of marital captivity in my bloodline!

Scripture: Isaiah 10:27

513.
I break off every spiritual wedding conducted in the realm of darkness—I divorce every spirit husband or wife NOW!

Scripture: Matthew 19:6

514.
I renounce every name, ring, or mark given to me by spirit spouses—be erased by the Blood of Jesus!

Scripture: Galatians 6:17

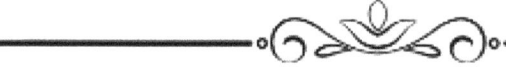

515.
I command spiritual freedom in my mind, emotions, and affections—I will no longer be manipulated by demonic bonds!

Scripture: Romans 12:2

516.
O Lord, restore purity, clarity, and stability in my relationships—let divine order reign!

Scripture: Psalm 37:23

517.
I release fire upon every dream altar where spiritual marriage covenants were renewed—scatter without remedy!

Scripture: Job 5:12

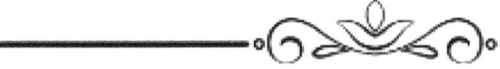

518.
Every serpent sent to defile my emotions, body, or sleep—come out and die by Holy Ghost fire!

Scripture: Luke 10:19

519.

I recover every opportunity, season, or favor lost due to spiritual marriage—let restoration come by divine speed!

Scripture: Amos 9:13

520.

I renounce the fear of marriage and the spirit of confusion concerning divine connection—Holy Spirit, take over!

Scripture: 2 Timothy 1:7

521.

Every demonic dream of wedding, union, or entanglement—I reject and reverse it by the Blood of Jesus!

Scripture: Matthew 13:25

522.

I declare: I am no longer bound to spirit spouses or ungodly ties—I am free, whole, and blessed in Christ Jesus!

Scripture: John 8:36

523.

Every marine altar calling my name or bloodline—be consumed by the fire of Jehovah and scatter beyond repair!

Scripture: Exodus 12:12

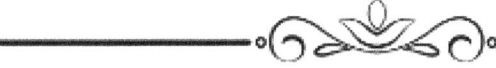

524.

I release thunder and lightning from the throne of God into every river, ocean, or stream where covenants were made—break by fire!

Scripture: Nahum 1:4

525.

Every spirit baby, spirit child, or spiritual responsibility forced upon me by marine powers—be aborted by Holy Ghost fire!

Scripture: Psalm 124:7

526.

I renounce and disconnect from every underwater covenant initiated in my dreams, through sex, or by ancestral dedication!

Scripture: 2 Corinthians 6:17

527.

O Lord, dry up every marine channel flowing into my life—no more interference, no more attacks!

Scripture: Isaiah 27:1

528.
I break every yoke of spiritual slavery to water spirits—let the rod of their oppression be shattered now!

Scripture: Isaiah 10:27

529.
Every demonic anchor linking my life to marine altars— be uprooted by the whirlwind of Jehovah!

Scripture: Jeremiah 51:1

530.
Let the thunder of God strike every mermaid, queen of the coast, and marine messenger assigned to my destiny!

Scripture: Psalm 29:7-9

SECTION NINETEEN: MISSILES TO CRUSH MARINE ALTARS, SPIRIT BABIES & UNDERWATER COVENANTS (PRAYERS 531–560)

Foundation Scripture:
"Thou shalt not suffer a witch to live."

— Exodus 22:18

531.

I cut off every cord, rope, or chain tying me to marine altars—I escape now by the Blood of Jesus!

Scripture: Zechariah 9:11

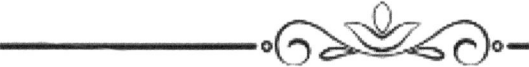

532.

Every evil deposit from the marine world in my body—be flushed out by Holy Ghost fire and divine power!

Scripture: Matthew 15:13

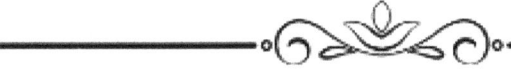

533.

I refuse to be manipulated, seduced, or deceived by marine spirits—I wear the armor of purity and light!

Scripture: Ephesians 6:11

534.

Let the fire of deliverance consume every marine charm, bracelet, or object in my possession—burn without mercy!

Scripture: Acts 19:19

535.

Every evil river flowing into my dreams—dry up now, I close the gate permanently by the Blood!

Scripture: Revelation 22:1

536.

I release Holy Ghost torpedoes into every underwater shrine, palace, and chamber where my destiny is being held—explode them now!

Scripture: Psalm 18:15

537.

I reject every spiritual marriage or agreement made in the waters—let divine divorce be issued by fire!

Scripture: Deuteronomy 12:2-3

538.

Every altar of the queen of the coast speaking against my progress—catch fire now and be buried in thunder!

Scripture: Psalm 74:13-14

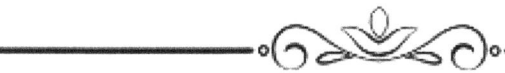

539.

I block every dream portal used by water spirits to manipulate my sleep—no more access, no more defilement!

Scripture: Job 33:15-16

540.

O God of fire, arise and burn every marine garment placed upon me—consume it until nothing remains!

Scripture: Zechariah 3:4

541.

I command the destruction of every evil calendar, registry, and identity programmed in the marine world using my name!

Scripture: Colossians 2:14

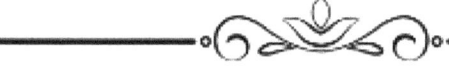

542.

Let the divine sword of Jehovah cut off every communication line between me and marine agents—I sever all links forever!

Scripture: Jeremiah 51:20

543.
I reverse every marine transaction performed against me, my children, or my spouse—be undone by the Blood of Jesus!

Scripture: Isaiah 44:25

544.
O Lord, send your angelic divers to retrieve every stolen virtue and destiny hidden beneath the waters—restore now!

Scripture: Isaiah 49:25

545.
I declare: I am not a property of the marine world—I belong to Jesus Christ alone!

Scripture: 1 Corinthians 6:20

546.
Let every snake spirit from the water realm tormenting my life—be roasted by Holy Ghost fire!

Scripture: Acts 28:5

547.
I reject every spiritual pregnancy from the marine world—be flushed out now by divine fire!

Scripture: Galatians 5:1

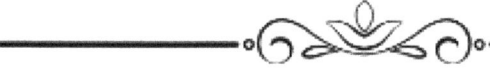

548.
Every marine power using my face, voice, or shadow—be exposed and destroyed without remedy!

Scripture: Psalm 27:2

549.
I break free from every spiritual identity assigned to me in the waters—my name is redeemed in Christ!

Scripture: Isaiah 62:2

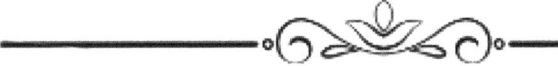

550.
Let the Blood of Jesus flood every marine altar bearing my name—overthrow it now in Jesus' name!

Scripture: Revelation 12:11

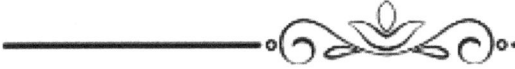

551.
I command the fire of Jehovah to melt every spiritual chain forged in the sea against my life—break and scatter!

Scripture: Psalm 107:14

552.

I decree: No marine altar, agent, or covenant shall ever rise again in my life—I am fire-branded and delivered forever!

Scripture: Obadiah 1:17

553.

O Lord, arise and scatter every witchcraft power delaying my marital destiny—let fire fall upon every stronghold!

Scripture: Isaiah 34:16

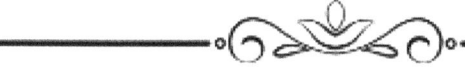

554.

Every covenant of marital delay, rejection, and denial—be broken now by the Blood of Jesus!

Scripture: Isaiah 10:27

555.
I release fire into the camp of every household enemy sitting on my marriage—be unseated by force!

Scripture: Psalm 35:4

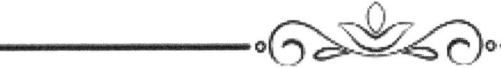

556.
Let every veil of invisibility covering me from my God-ordained spouse—catch fire and burn to ashes!

Scripture: Isaiah 25:7

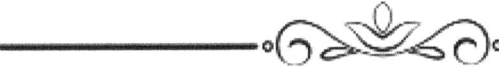

557.
I command divine exposure and positioning—let my covenant partner locate me without delay!

Scripture: Genesis 24:12-15

558.

Every spirit spouse monitoring and blocking my marital glory—be arrested and cast out by Holy Ghost fire!

Scripture: Isaiah 54:5

559.

I disconnect from every counterfeit relationship sent to distract, delay, or destroy my marriage destiny!

Scripture: 2 Corinthians 6:14

560.

Let the lightning of God destroy every altar of marital failure in my father's and mother's house!

Scripture: Judges 6:25

SECTION TWENTY: MISSILES FOR MARITAL BREAKTHROUGH, DIVINE CONNECTION & RESTORATION (PRAYERS 561–620)

Foundation Scripture:
"Thou shalt not suffer a witch to live."

– Exodus 22:18

561.
Every soul tie with past relationships draining my virtue—
be broken now by the Blood of Jesus!

Scripture: Galatians 5:1

562.
O God, restore my dignity, my favor, and my divine
attractiveness—let marital doors open with speed!

Scripture: Psalm 90:17

563.
I reject the spirit of bitterness, fear, and discouragement—
Holy Spirit, prepare me for divine connection!

Scripture: 2 Timothy 1:7

564.
Every prophecy of late marriage, repeated heartbreak, or loneliness—be cancelled by the mercy of God!

Scripture: Zephaniah 3:17

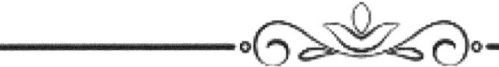

565.
I release the sword of the Lord to break every padlock and chain holding my marital breakthrough!

Scripture: Psalm 107:16

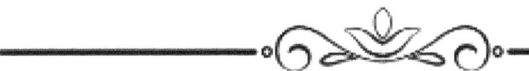

566.
Let every monitoring mirror, spell, or charm against my relationship life—be shattered now in Jesus' name!

Scripture: Numbers 23:23

567.

O Lord, redirect my steps to align with Your perfect will for marriage—no more confusion!

Scripture: Psalm 32:8

568.

I silence every voice of error that led me into past wrong relationships—be muted forever!

Scripture: Proverbs 3:5-6

569.

Every altar of polygamy, adultery, or spiritual sabotage—be dismantled by the power of the Holy Ghost!

Scripture: Malachi 2:15-16

570.
O Lord, restore every lost virtue, time, and opportunity in my marital journey—let divine compensation flow!

Scripture: Joel 2:25

571.
Let every spirit of jealousy and envy attacking my marital breakthrough—be destroyed by fire!

Scripture: Psalm 27:2

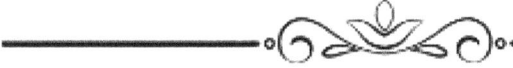

572.
I decree: My marriage shall be a testimony of fire, purity, and fulfillment—it shall not be delayed or hijacked!

Scripture: Proverbs 18:22

573.
O God arise, reveal and remove every counterfeit that looks like the real—let only divine alignment remain!

Scripture: Matthew 7:15-16

574.
I cover my future spouse, home, and union with the Blood of Jesus—no power shall infiltrate or divide!

Scripture: Matthew 19:6

575.
Let every demonic seed of confusion, strife, or misunderstanding in my current or future relationship—be uprooted by fire!

Scripture: Amos 3:3

576.
I bind every spirit of seduction and sexual manipulation sent to destroy marital destinies—be cast out now!

Scripture: 1 Thessalonians 4:3-5

577.
I call forth God-ordained covenant partners for my children—no marine, demonic, or counterfeit link shall prevail!

Scripture: Psalm 112:2

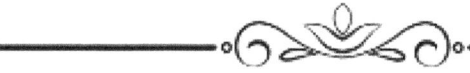

578.
Every evil name given to my relationship status in the spirit—be erased and replaced with divine favor!

Scripture: Isaiah 62:2

579.

Let the handwriting of loneliness, bitterness, and delay be wiped off by the Blood of Jesus!

Scripture: Colossians 2:14

580.

O Lord, breathe life into every area of my emotions and heart—restore joy, trust, and expectation!

Scripture: Psalm 51:10-12

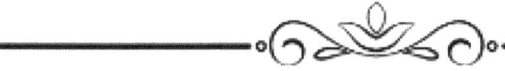

581.

I declare supernatural alignment in my marital journey—I shall not miss my season again!

Scripture: Ecclesiastes 3:11

582.

I decree: My marriage shall glorify God, fulfill destiny, and stand strong—no witch or altar shall stop it!

Scripture: 1 Corinthians 13:13

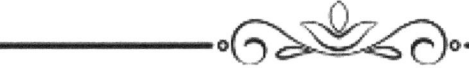

583.

Every spiritual embargo placed upon my marriage by ancestral or witchcraft altars— scatter by thunder and the Blood of Jesus!

Scripture: Isaiah 10:27

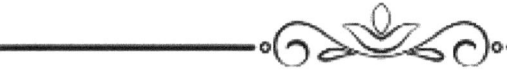

584.

I command the spirit of late marriage, confusion, and disappointment—expire now by the fire of God and judgment in the Blood!

Scripture: Psalm 68:6

585.
O Lord, send the sword of fire into every satanic cage holding my divine partner or marriage—break and release by force!

Scripture: Isaiah 49:25

586.
Every covenant of bitterness, delay, or marital rejection—be broken by the Blood of Jesus and reversed forever!

Scripture: Zechariah 9:11

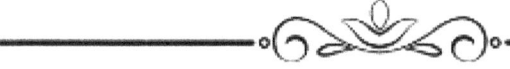

587.
I release atomic bomb prayers into every witchcraft mirror monitoring my marital joy—shatter by fire now!

Scripture: Job 5:12

588.
Let the altar of Jehovah speak against every strange voice manipulating my spouse or relationship—be silenced forever!

Scripture: Hebrews 12:24

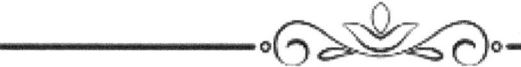

589.
O God of Elijah, burn every spiritual certificate of demotion issued against my marriage—let it turn to ashes!

Scripture: Deuteronomy 7:5

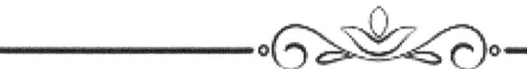

590.
I invoke Holy Ghost thunder to locate every agent of delay, seduction, and manipulation assigned to scatter my union—be wasted!

Scripture: Psalm 18:14

591.
Every soul tie with counterfeit relationships—break now by the Blood of Jesus and divine separation!

Scripture: 2 Corinthians 6:14

592.
I cancel every evil marital pattern of divorce, separation, and betrayal—my story shall be different!

Scripture: Isaiah 43:19

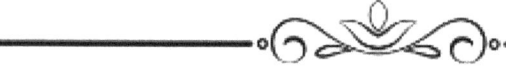

593.
Let angels of divine favor announce my marital restoration and breakthrough—divine connection manifest now!

Scripture: Proverbs 18:22

594.
I declare the gates of my marriage open by fire—no demon shall shut what God has ordained!

Scripture: Revelation 3:8

595.
O consuming fire, visit my marriage, and burn every serpent hiding in trust, communication, and intimacy!

Scripture: Luke 10:19

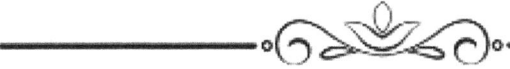

596.
Every voice of delay and marital manipulation from evil altars—be silenced by the Blood of Jesus!

Scripture: Lamentations 3:37

597.
I break free from every past relationship acting as a spiritual spouse in the dream—fire of God, consume them!

Scripture: Matthew 15:13

598.
O Lord, crown my marriage with favor, peace, unity, and fire—no power shall scatter it again!

Scripture: Ecclesiastes 4:12

599.
O Lord, arise as Jehovah El Gibbor and strike down every witchcraft mirror monitoring my family—shatter them beyond repair!

Scripture: Isaiah 42:13

600.

I plead the Blood of Jesus Christ, the Lamb that was slain, against every evil eye following my steps—be blinded forever!

Scripture: Zechariah 2:5

601.

I decree marital joy, fruitfulness, and divine covering over my household—in Jesus' name!

Scripture: Psalm 128:1-3

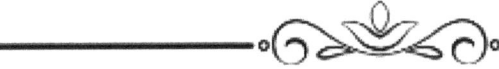

602.

O Lord, arise and destroy every satanic altar calling my womb barren—let fire answer now!

Scripture: Exodus 23:26

603.

Every demonic padlock placed on my womb, seed, or fruitfulness—break and scatter in the name of Jesus!

Scripture: Isaiah 22:22

604.

I command every seed of affliction, infertility, and delay in my reproductive system—burn by the fire of the Holy Ghost!

Scripture: Malachi 4:2

605.

O God of Hannah, answer me with fire and fruitfulness—give me testimony beyond medical expectation!

Scripture: 1 Samuel 1:27

606.
Let angelic surgeons visit my womb or system now—
perform divine repair and restoration!

Scripture: Jeremiah 30:17

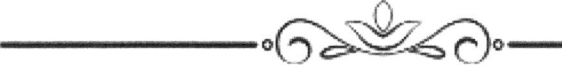

607.
I claim my season of conception—what was impossible
before shall now become my testimony!

Scripture: Genesis 21:1-2

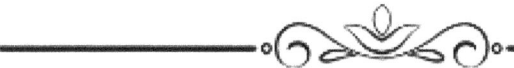

608.
Every evil covenant of sorrow, miscarriage, and shame—
be broken and buried now by fire!

Scripture: 2 Samuel 22:30

609.

I reject every dream of miscarriage, stillbirth, or abortion—I cancel it by the Blood of Jesus!

Scripture: Psalm 91:10

610.

I cover my womb, my children, and every pregnancy connected to me with the Blood of Jesus!

Scripture: Revelation 12:11

611.

Every demonic object blocking fruitfulness—melt and vanish by fire and the Word of the Lord!

Scripture: Jeremiah 23:29

612.
I recover every stolen egg, seed, or child taken through spiritual manipulation—restore now!

Scripture: Isaiah 49:25

613.
O Lord, rewrite my biological report—let the impossible become a miracle!

Scripture: Luke 1:37

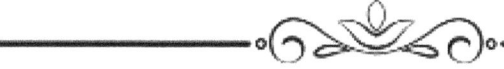

614.
I declare my womb is blessed, fruitful, and protected—I shall carry full-term and deliver safely!

Scripture: Deuteronomy 28:4

615.
I come against every household altar that declares "none shall conceive"—scatter now and be destroyed!

Scripture: Numbers 23:23

616.
Let divine conception rest upon me and every woman believing for fruitfulness—release power now!

Scripture: Luke 1:35

617.
I command every marine, ancestral, or witchcraft spirit assigned to cause barrenness—be arrested now!

Scripture: Isaiah 27:1

618.
I release fire on every evil padlock placed over my reproductive life—break and never return!

Scripture: Isaiah 22:22

619.
I soak every month, trimester, and delivery date in the Blood of Jesus—no attack shall prosper!

Scripture: Psalm 121:7-8

620.
I declare: I shall carry my evidence, my testimony, my miracle child(ren)—no altar or affliction shall stop me!

Scripture: Psalm 126:5-6

SECTION TWENTY-TWO: MISSILES TO DESTROY WITCHCRAFT DELAY, DIVINE HELPERS BLOCKAGE & ANTI-FAVOR ALTARS (PRAYERS 621–650)

Foundation Scripture:
"Thou shalt not suffer a witch to live."

— Exodus 22:18

621.
Every witchcraft chain tying down my destiny helpers—break now by fire and let divine connection be restored!

Scripture: Isaiah 60:10

622.
I release the sword of the Lord against every power blocking the faces of my helpers—let their scales fall off by fire!

Scripture: Acts 9:18

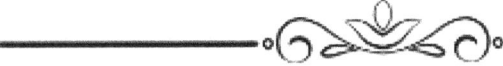

623.
O Lord, release thunder from Heaven to scatter every altar of anti-favor erected against my name!

Scripture: Psalm 44:3

624.

Every spirit of delay assigned to slow down my helpers or disconnect them from me—be arrested now by the Blood of Jesus!

Scripture: Daniel 10:13

625.

Let every evil voice misrepresenting me in the ears of those sent to favor me—be silenced by Holy Ghost fire!

Scripture: Proverbs 16:7

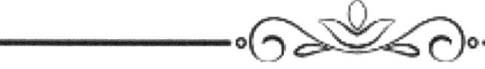

626.

I command the whirlwind of God to blow away every demonic fog hiding me from divine recognition!

Scripture: Isaiah 25:7

627.
Every satanic gate blocking my favor, access, and divine promotion—be lifted now in the name of Jesus!

Scripture: Psalm 24:7

628.
I summon the fire of Elijah against every personality standing between me and my next level of help!

Scripture: 2 Kings 1:10

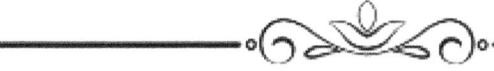

629.
Let the fire of favor fall upon my name, voice, gifts, and assignments—let doors open without resistance!

Scripture: Esther 2:17

630.

I command every anti-favor spell, curse, or incantation to break now and release me into divine visibility!

Scripture: Isaiah 61:7

631.

O Lord, raise prophetic voices to speak into my destiny and draw the attention of my appointed helpers!

Scripture: 1 Kings 17:9

632.

I decree my life shall no longer suffer rejection, forgetfulness, or delay—I am remembered by fire!

Scripture: Esther 6:1-3

633.
Every demonic detour assigned to mislead my helpers—scatter by fire, let alignment be restored!

Scripture: Psalm 37:23

634.
I reject the garment of disfavor, confusion, and shame—be consumed and replaced with honor!

Scripture: Isaiah 61:3

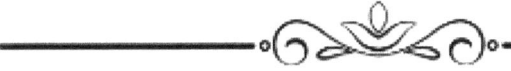

635.
Every altar of "not yet" programmed against my help and favor—scatter beyond repair!

Scripture: Ecclesiastes 3:11

636.

I speak to the north, south, east, and west—release my divine helpers now without delay!

Scripture: Isaiah 43:6

637.

O Lord, let divine speed and urgent favor overtake me—let my files be moved to the top now!

Scripture: Psalm 102:13

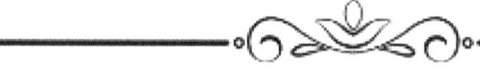

638.

Every demonic court where my name was sentenced to delay and denial—let divine mercy speak and overrule!

Scripture: Romans 8:33

639.

I command my name to be echoed in places of help, visibility, and strategic destiny advancement!

Scripture: Genesis 41:14

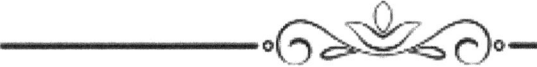

640.

Every demonic traffic jam on my path of favor and open doors—be cleared by the angel of fire!

Scripture: Exodus 23:20

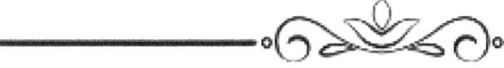

641.

Let the divine winds of God carry my name to those positioned to bless, promote, and elevate me!

Scripture: Proverbs 3:4

642.
I reject delay in divine help—I walk into early manifestation of answered prayers!

Scripture: Isaiah 65:24

643.
Every altar of manipulation keeping me in waiting mode—catch fire and collapse now!

Scripture: Micah 7:7

644.
Let every anti-favor personality be exposed and permanently removed from my life!

Scripture: Proverbs 26:27

645.

I am surrounded by favor like a shield—no more dry seasons, no more missed appointments!

Scripture: Psalm 5:12

646.

Let divine resources, sponsorship, and strategic partners begin to locate me daily!

Scripture: Philippians 4:19

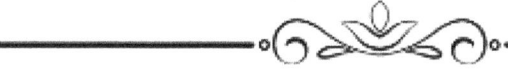

647.

I reject every delay in financial release, recommendation, and approval—let divine release manifest now!

Scripture: Deuteronomy 28:12

648.

Let favor, mercy, and divine remembrance collide in my life—my name shall echo in the right places!

Scripture: Luke 1:30

649.

I decree and declare: From this day forward, helpers shall rise for me daily and without delay!

Scripture: Psalm 121:2

650.

Every enemy of divine help, every architect of stagnation—expire by thunder in the name of Jesus Christ!

Scripture: Isaiah 54:17

SECTION TWENTY-THREE:

MISSILES AGAINST WITCHCRAFT MANIPULATION, DESTINY DIVERSION & CONFUSION

Prayers 651–680

Foundation Scripture:
"Thou shalt not suffer a witch to live."

– Exodus 22:18

651.

Every witchcraft agenda designed to manipulate my destiny—catch fire and be destroyed without mercy!

Scripture: 2 Kings 1:10

652.

I scatter every altar of confusion, mental oppression, and spiritual diversion targeting my path!

Scripture: 1 Corinthians 14:33

653.

Every arrow of destiny diversion fired against my calling—backfire now in the name of Jesus!

Scripture: Isaiah 30:21

654.
I command every spell, charm, or sacrifice aimed at changing my original assignment—be reversed by fire!

Scripture: Psalm 91:13

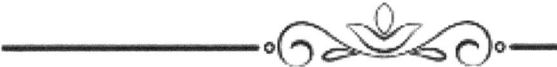

655.
O Lord, restore my feet to the path of prophetic accuracy—no more spiritual wandering!

Scripture: Psalm 37:23

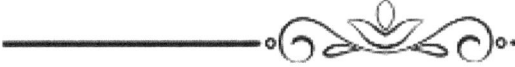

656.
I bind the spirit of double-mindedness, spiritual blindness, and demonic confusion—be cast out by fire!

Scripture: James 1:8

657.
Let the anointing for discernment and divine precision fall upon me afresh—no more satanic detours!

Scripture: Proverbs 3:5-6

658.
Every voice of manipulation whispering lies to my soul— be silenced by the Blood of Jesus!

Scripture: 2 Timothy 1:7

659.
I revoke every demonic appointment and relationship assigned to derail my life—be terminated by thunder!

Scripture: Matthew 15:13

660.

Every delay tactic used to trap me in the wrong place at the wrong time—scatter by fire and thunder!

Scripture: Ecclesiastes 3:1

661.

I destroy every demonic blueprint drafted to misalign my destiny—burn now in Jesus' name!

Scripture: Isaiah 8:10

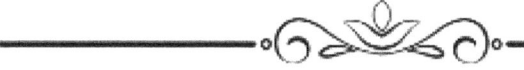

662.

Let every evil counselor or advisor assigned to manipulate my choices—be exposed and removed by fire!

Scripture: Psalm 1:1

663.

I call forth divine mentors, kingdom voices, and wise counsel to guide me in alignment with Heaven!

Scripture: Proverbs 11:14

664.

Every attack on my spiritual accuracy—be reversed by the fire of God and prophetic correction!

Scripture: Jeremiah 1:9-10

665.

I cancel every manipulation of dreams, visions, and revelations—let my spiritual sight be restored!

Scripture: Joel 2:28

666.
I declare: I shall not be misled, deceived, or manipulated—I walk in the light of God's Word!

Scripture: Psalm 119:105

667.
O God, realign my relationships, assignments, and movements with divine timing and direction!

Scripture: Romans 8:14

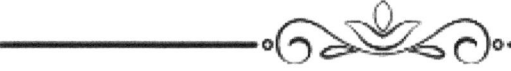

668.
I destroy every witchcraft mirror, screen, or portal used to control my decisions—shatter by fire now!

Scripture: Isaiah 44:25

669.
Let the altar of clarity and revelation be raised in my life—confusion shall not rule me again!

Scripture: Ephesians 1:17-18

670.
Every dark veil cast over my mind and direction—tear now in the name of Jesus!

Scripture: 2 Corinthians 3:16

671.
I command spiritual accuracy and prophetic sharpness to locate me—no more guessing or delays!

Scripture: Isaiah 30:21

672.

Every evil river pulling me off course—dry up and disappear by the sword of the Lord!

Scripture: Psalm 29:10

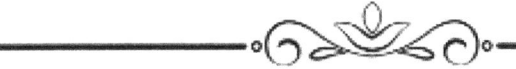

673.

I declare judgment against destiny kidnappers, soul manipulators, and demonic influencers—perish now!

Scripture: Psalm 7:15-16

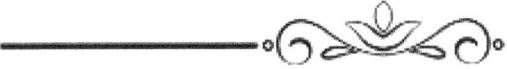

674.

Every satanic seat of control established in my soul—be uprooted now by the power in the Blood!

Scripture: Galatians 5:1

675.

I reject every counterfeit assignment and satanic appointment—only the will of God shall stand in my life!

Scripture: Romans 12:2

676.

I release atomic bombs against every dream of misdirection, confusion, and spiritual deception—scatter now!

Scripture: Job 33:15-16

677.

Let the sword of light destroy every spiritual fog cast over my purpose and journey!

Scripture: John 8:12

678.

Every ancient voice of misguidance in my bloodline—be silenced by fire and divine light!

Scripture: Proverbs 4:18

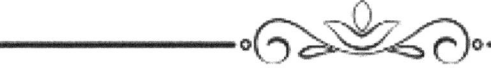

679.

O Lord, reset my path with divine GPS—realign me with Your prophecy and direction!

Scripture: Psalm 23:3

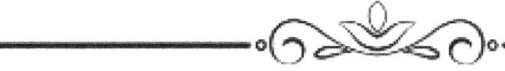

680.

I declare total freedom from every form of spiritual manipulation, mental fog, and destiny detour—IN JESUS' NAME!

Scripture: John 8:36

SECTION TWENTY-FOUR: MISSILES TO TEAR DOWN SATANIC THRONES, ANCESTRAL KINGSHIPS & BLOODLINE DOMINIONS (PRAYERS 681–710)

Foundation Scripture:
"Thou shalt not suffer a witch to live."

— Exodus 22:18

681.

Every satanic throne seated over my father's house—be overthrown by thunder and fire!

Scripture: Obadiah 1:21

682.

I pull down every ancestral kingship exalting itself against my rising—scatter without mercy!

Scripture: 2 Corinthians 10:4-5

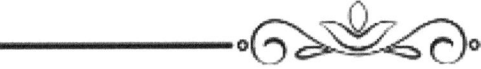

683.

Every ruler of darkness in my bloodline—be dethroned and buried by the Blood of Jesus!

Scripture: Colossians 2:15

684.

I release divine earthquake into every hidden throneroom of darkness where my name is summoned—let it collapse now!

Scripture: Psalm 18:7

685.

Let the crown of ancestral dominion be removed from every demonic ruler in my lineage—be destroyed without remedy!

Scripture: Lamentations 5:16

686.

O Lord, let fire fall upon every satanic elder council resisting my generation's breakthrough!

Scripture: Isaiah 28:14-18

687.

Every altar of generational rulership opposing kingdom advancement in my life—scatter now by fire!

Scripture: Exodus 15:3

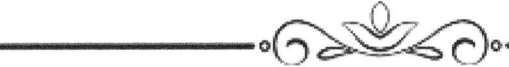

688.

I release the rod of iron upon every demonic royal seat inherited in my family—break into pieces now!

Scripture: Psalm 2:9

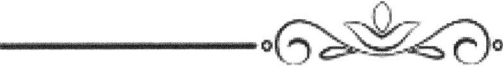

689.

Every evil throne manipulating my inheritance—catch fire and be permanently dismantled!

Scripture: Jeremiah 1:10

690.

O Lord, arise and tear every veil hiding satanic kings ruling behind the scenes—expose and destroy them!

Scripture: Job 34:21-22

691.

I call for angelic battalions to invade and dislodge every ruler of ancestral oppression in my lineage!

Scripture: Psalm 103:20

692.

Every demonic monarch enforcing witchcraft in my father's or mother's house—fall and perish by fire!

Scripture: Isaiah 47:1-3

693.
Let the thunder of God unseat every spirit reigning illegally over my life—no more false dominion!

Scripture: Revelation 11:15

694.
I declare judgment against every ancient throne resisting my elevation—scatter now and be forgotten!

Scripture: Isaiah 14:12-15

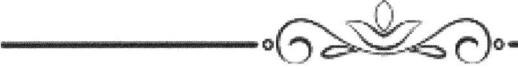

695.
Every throne of sickness, delay, poverty, or confusion—be removed from my family by the sword of fire!

Scripture: Jeremiah 10:11

696.
O God, arise and shake every demonic palace controlling regional destinies—let their pillars collapse!

Scripture: Judges 16:29-30

697.
Every bloodline covenant that enthroned darkness in my generation—break now by the Blood of the Everlasting Covenant!

Scripture: Hebrews 13:20

698.
Let the scepter of righteousness displace every satanic scepter lifted against my household!

Scripture: Hebrews 1:8

699.

I pronounce the downfall of every territorial ruler standing as Pharaoh over my destiny—let them drown in their own Red Sea!

Scripture: Exodus 14:27-28

700.

Every false dominion exerted over my mind, health, finances, or calling—be broken by the power of the Holy Ghost!

Scripture: Romans 6:14

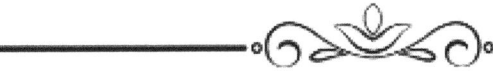

701.

I strip every ancestral entity of its influence and authority in my generation—no more rulership, no more control!

Scripture: Isaiah 25:7

702.

I declare my bloodline cleansed of every throne of rebellion, witchcraft, and serpentine influence!

Scripture: Ezekiel 36:26

703.

Every power that claimed ownership over my family tree—be cut off and cast into outer darkness!

Scripture: Matthew 15:13

704.

I release judgment fire against every foundational king and queen who swore to oppose my rising—scatter now!

Scripture: 2 Kings 9:22-33

705.

Let every seat of ancient power in my village, territory, or ancestry—be removed by divine force!

Scripture: Jeremiah 51:25

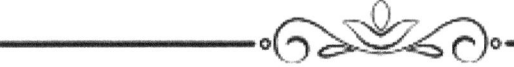

706.

I reject every crown of shame, delay, and affliction—let it be burned and replaced with the crown of glory!

Scripture: Isaiah 61:3

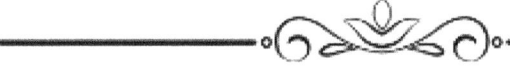

707.

I stand in my rightful inheritance and declare: I rule and reign with Christ Jesus—no more demonic interference!

Scripture: Revelation 5:10

708.
Let every spirit of Herod and Nebuchadnezzar opposing my star—be cut off suddenly by the hand of God!

Scripture: Acts 12:21-23

709.
I take back my throne of glory, honor, and purpose—no satanic king shall sit where I am ordained to rule!

Scripture: Revelation 3:21

710.
I decree: every satanic throne, dominion, or rulership over my life and generation is permanently overthrown—IN JESUS' NAME!

Scripture: Colossians 2:15

SECTION TWENTY-FIVE: MISSILES TO SECURE DELIVERANCE FROM THE PIT, CURSES & SPIRITUAL SLAVERY (PRAYERS 711–740)

Foundation Scripture:
"Thou shalt not suffer a witch to live."

– Exodus 22:18

711.

O Lord, pull me out of every spiritual pit where my destiny has been buried—let resurrection power speak now!

Scripture: Psalm 40:2

712.

I break free from every cage, pit, and spiritual prison—let the gates open by fire!

Scripture: Acts 12:7

713.

Every generational curse holding me in cycles of limitation—break now by the Blood of Jesus!

Scripture: Galatians 3:13

714.
I release Holy Ghost fire against every chain of slavery, affliction, and delay—scatter beyond repair!

Scripture: Isaiah 10:27

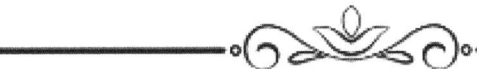

715.
O God arise, let the cords of the wicked be cut off from my destiny—no more bondage!

Scripture: Psalm 129:4

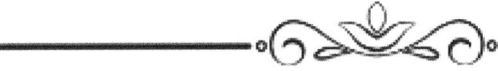

716.
I reject spiritual imprisonment—I walk in liberty by the anointing of the Holy Ghost!

Scripture: 2 Corinthians 3:17

717.

Every pit of shame, failure, and backwardness dug for me—swallow the digger now!

Scripture: Proverbs 26:27

718.

I break every invisible shackle tying me to past mistakes and failures—let the Blood of Jesus wash it away!

Scripture: Revelation 12:11

719.

Every spiritual slave master assigned to torment my destiny—be dethroned and destroyed by fire!

Scripture: Exodus 14:13

720.

Let the sword of the Lord cut off every rope of manipulation dragging me into old patterns!

Scripture: Jeremiah 30:8

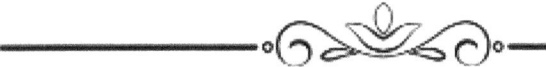

721.

I arise from every grave where my destiny, voice, or name was buried—let resurrection power speak!

Scripture: Ezekiel 37:12

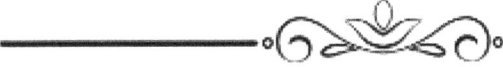

722.

Every altar calling my name back into captivity—be silenced and shattered forever!

Scripture: Psalm 124:7

723.

I declare: I am not a spiritual slave—I am a blood-bought child of God!

Scripture: John 8:36

724.

Let every generational pit of rejection and abandonment collapse by the power of the Most High!

Scripture: Isaiah 61:7

725.

Every dark chain forged through ancestral rituals—be broken by the fire of deliverance!

Scripture: Numbers 23:23

726.
I recover every virtue, glory, and spiritual strength stolen through captivity—be restored by fire!

Scripture: Joel 2:25

727.
O Lord, let every pit keeper assigned to hold me down be consumed by the fire they planned for me!

Scripture: Daniel 6:24

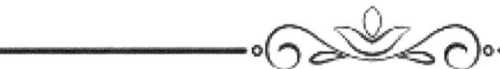

728.
I cancel every curse that says I will not rise, build, or prosper—be nullified by the Blood of Jesus!

Scripture: Deuteronomy 28:13

729.

Let the mighty arm of God pull me out of every hole of obscurity, delay, and failure!

Scripture: Isaiah 41:10

730.

I decree: I will not die in any satanic pit—I rise by the power of Jesus Christ!

Scripture: Psalm 118:17

731.

Every spell, vow, or evil word spoken to imprison my star—be broken and reversed now!

Scripture: Isaiah 8:10

732.
Let every monitoring spirit assigned to report my movement back to the pit—go blind and be destroyed!

Scripture: 2 Kings 6:18

733.
I command fire to consume every ancestral curse of delay, hardship, and premature loss!

Scripture: Obadiah 1:17

734.
O God, shine Your light on every hidden chain still holding any part of me—let it be exposed and shattered!

Scripture: Luke 8:17

735.
I break the covenant of spiritual slavery—I enter covenant with freedom, power, and victory!

Scripture: Hebrews 8:6

736.
Let divine visitation come to every family member still trapped in spiritual prisons—be loosed by fire!

Scripture: Psalm 102:19-20

737.
I declare: No curse shall succeed in my life—I am a breaker, a builder, and a child of destiny!

Scripture: Numbers 23:20

738.

Every satanic pit dug for my health, marriage, ministry, or finances—collapse and bury your owner!

Scripture: Psalm 7:15-16

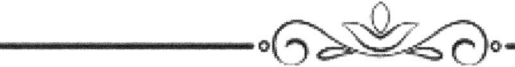

739.

O Lord, lift me out of every condition, cycle, or place that mocks my covenant with You—elevate me by grace!

Scripture: Psalm 3:3

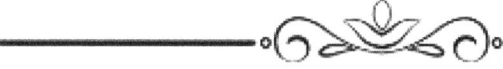

740.

I declare: I walk in liberty, power, and dominion—no more bondage, no more backwardness, no more fear!

Scripture: 2 Timothy 1:7

SECTION TWENTY-SIX: MISSILES TO COMMAND MIDNIGHT BREAKTHROUGHS, ANGELIC RELEASE & PROPHETIC SHIFTS

(PRAYERS 741–770)

Foundation Scripture:
"Thou shalt not suffer a witch to live."

— Exodus 22:18

741.

O Lord, let the gates of midnight open for my breakthrough—let angelic intervention be released suddenly!

Scripture: Acts 16:25-26

742.

Every power that awakens at midnight to invoke delay, disaster, or death—be destroyed by thunder and fire!

Scripture: Psalm 91:5-6

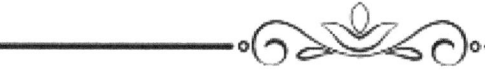

743.

I command every chained breakthrough to be loosed tonight—I release fire upon every padlock!

Scripture: Isaiah 45:2-3

744.

O God of midnight, arise and silence every voice rising in judgment against me while I sleep!

Scripture: Isaiah 54:17

745.

Let the angels assigned to enforce my deliverance be activated now—arrest every demon on duty!

Scripture: Psalm 34:7

746.

I call forth midnight rain of favor, promotion, and restoration—let it fall upon me now without hindrance!

Scripture: Job 29:6

747.
Every witchcraft agenda assigned to be fulfilled in the night—be cut off by fire before it manifests!

Scripture: Exodus 12:29-30

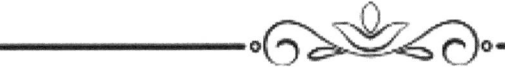

748.
I decree divine reversal over every demonic declaration spoken over me while I was asleep—reverse by fire!

Scripture: Lamentations 3:37

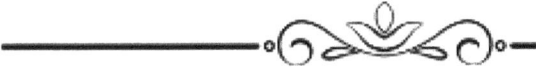

749.
Let the fire of the Holy Ghost consume every shadow spirit walking through my home at midnight!

Scripture: Psalm 35:5-6

750.

I scatter every meeting of witches, marine agents, and enchanters that gather by night—scatter by thunder!

Scripture: Psalm 68:1-2

751.

O Lord, let my midnight praise provoke angelic jailbreaks for every locked blessing in my life!

Scripture: Acts 16:25-26

752.

I decree supernatural downloads, prophetic encounters, and divine instructions to be released in the midnight hour!

Scripture: Job 33:15-16

753.
Let every altar summoning me at midnight—collapse now by the sword of the Lord!

Scripture: Judges 6:25

754.
I command a prophetic shift to take place in my life from this night forward—let divine realignment begin!

Scripture: Isaiah 43:19

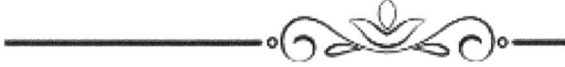

755.
Every python spirit sent to swallow my midnight fire—be roasted alive and never rise again!

Scripture: Acts 16:16-18

756.

I release atomic missiles into every territory where my voice has been silenced—let my sound break out now!

Scripture: Psalm 29:3-5

757.

Let every spiritual embargo on my prayers and progress be lifted as I war in the midnight hour!

Scripture: Daniel 10:12-13

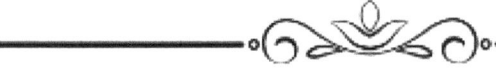

758.

O Lord, let my midnight declarations shake altars, expose enemies, and usher in divine justice!

Scripture: Psalm 149:6-9

759.

Every ancient power that operates in my dreams and midnight hour—perish now by the Blood of Jesus!

Scripture: Revelation 12:11

760.

I decree open heavens over my midnight warfare—let divine secrets and blueprints be revealed to me!

Scripture: Jeremiah 33:3

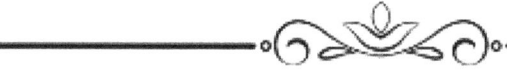

761.

I command a change in the realm of the spirit—let every invisible resistance be pulled down!

Scripture: 2 Corinthians 10:4

762.
I break into my next season by fire—let every old chain snap at the voice of midnight praise!

Scripture: Isaiah 10:27

763.
Let the trumpet of breakthrough sound over my name tonight—every wall must fall!

Scripture: Joshua 6:20

764.
O God of sudden shifts, shake the foundations of delay, stagnation, and failure in my life!

Scripture: Haggai 2:6-9

765.

I receive divine speed, direction, and clarity from tonight's midnight watch—I shall not miss it!

Scripture: Psalm 119:105

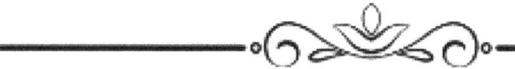

766.

I release judgment missiles against midnight arrows—every arrow of sickness, fear, or confusion—backfire!

Scripture: Psalm 91:5

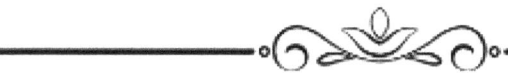

767.

Let angelic fire sweep through my home, region, and territory—cleanse every trace of darkness!

Scripture: Psalm 18:14

768.
I speak prophetic turnaround over my life—I wake up into divine results, resources, and rejoicing!

Scripture: Psalm 30:5

769.
O Lord, let this night mark the end of delay and the beginning of divine manifestations!

Scripture: Isaiah 60:22

770.
I declare: My midnight prayer is not in vain. Let my testimony arise, and my enemies fall—IN JESUS' NAME!

Scripture: Psalm 118:17

SECTION TWENTY-SEVEN: MISSILES TO DISMANTLE WITCHCRAFT SURVEILLANCE, SPIRITUAL ESPIONAGE & DREAM INVASION (PRAYERS 771–800)

Foundation Scripture:
"Thou shalt not suffer a witch to live."

– Exodus 22:18

771.
Every spiritual camera, mirror, and monitoring altar watching my movements—be shattered now by fire!

Scripture: Isaiah 44:25

772.
I blind every evil eye and shut down every witchcraft watcher assigned to track my progress!

Scripture: 2 Kings 6:18

773.
O Lord, hide me in Your glory cloud—let no demon or sorcerer detect my breakthrough!

Scripture: Psalm 91:1

774.

Every demonic frequency broadcasting my information into satanic networks—be jammed and scattered!

Scripture: Job 5:12

775.

Let the Blood of Jesus cover my name, voice, image, and shadow—no tracking system shall find me again!

Scripture: Revelation 12:11

776.

Every household witchcraft mirror used to spy on me—break irreparably in the name of Jesus!

Scripture: Micah 7:6

777.
I release atomic fire into every coven that has taken interest in my destiny—burn now without mercy!

Scripture: Psalm 35:4-6

778.
Every familiar spirit following me around—lose your hold and disappear by thunder!

Scripture: Leviticus 20:27

779.
I disconnect my name from every spiritual journal, registry, or witchcraft database—be erased by fire!

Scripture: Colossians 2:14

780.

Let divine confusion strike every demonic surveillance camp assigned to my calling!

Scripture: Genesis 11:6-8

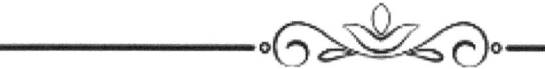

781.

I reverse every dream where my secrets were stolen, copied, or traded—restore now by the Blood of Jesus!

Scripture: Joel 2:25

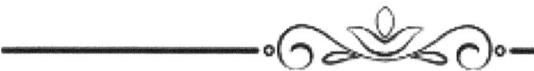

782.

Every night caterer feeding me demonic food in dreams—catch fire and perish by judgment!

Scripture: Matthew 15:13

783.

Let the sword of the Lord pursue every astral projector, spirit traveler, or marine observer visiting me at night!

Scripture: Psalm 35:5-6

784.

I declare my dream life is a no-fly zone for demons, agents, and evil personalities—entry is forbidden by fire!

Scripture: Job 33:15-16

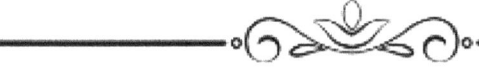

785.

I cover my bed, pillow, and sleep realm with the Blood of Jesus—no witch shall cross the line!

Scripture: Exodus 12:13

786.

Let every serpent, dog, or animal sent in the dream realm be consumed by Holy Ghost fire!

Scripture: Luke 10:19

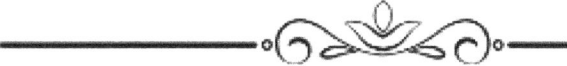

787.

I release fire upon every marine gate opened through dream manipulation—be sealed permanently!

Scripture: Revelation 3:7

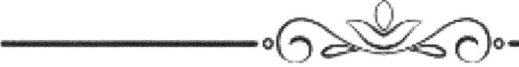

788.

Every invisible screen or mirror used to watch my prayers, plans, and progress—be broken in Jesus' name!

Scripture: Isaiah 8:10

789.
I erase my name, family, and address from every demonic map, radar, or spiritual GPS system!

Scripture: Zechariah 2:5

790.
I decree Holy Ghost fire upon every coven or cult that mentions me in rituals—scatter beyond recovery!

Scripture: Psalm 118:12

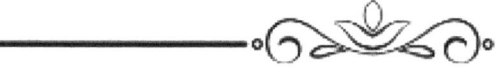

791.
Let thunder strike every evil observer standing at the gates of my breakthrough—fall down now!

Scripture: Psalm 29:7

792.

I reject every dream where I was summoned to court, shrines, or evil gatherings—cancelled by the Blood of Jesus!

Scripture: Lamentations 3:37

793.

Let every dream of delay, confusion, or false prophecy be erased by divine revelation!

Scripture: Jeremiah 23:29

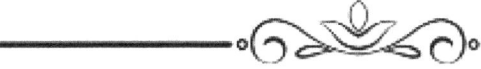

794.

I cancel every assignment of witchcraft impersonation in my dreams—my identity is fire-sealed!

Scripture: Isaiah 54:17

795.
I shut down every satanic lab where my photos, hair, or information has been programmed!

Scripture: Deuteronomy 18:10-12

796.
I summon the fire of God to pursue every dark spirit sent to gather intel from my dreams—burn now!

Scripture: Psalm 97:3

797.
Every scroll, file, or demonic folder bearing my name—be consumed in divine flames!

Scripture: Jeremiah 1:10

798.

I bind and cast out every serpent spirit that invades my night season—out by fire and thunder!

Scripture: Mark 16:17

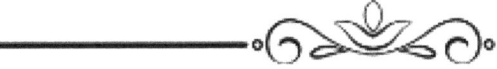

799.

O Lord, command Your angels to surround me while I sleep—let my dreams become altars of revelation and victory!

Scripture: Psalm 91:11

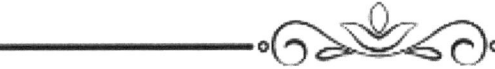

800.

I decree: From this day forward, my dreams shall be guarded, my secrets shall be hidden, and my enemies shall be silenced—IN JESUS' NAME!

Scripture: Job 22:28

SECTION TWENTY-EIGHT: MISSILES TO BREAK CHAINS OF AFFLICTION, LONG-TERM BATTLES & STUBBORN CONDITIONS (PRAYERS 801–830)

Foundation Scripture:
"Thou shalt not suffer a witch to live."

— Exodus 22:18

801.
O Lord, arise and terminate every long-term affliction mocking my prayers—scatter it now by fire!

Scripture: Nahum 1:9

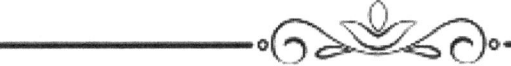

802
. I release atomic missiles against every generational sickness programmed into my bloodline—be flushed out by the Blood of Jesus!

Scripture: Jeremiah 30:17

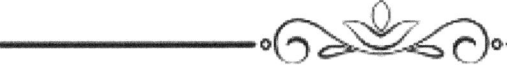

803.
Every satanic anchor holding my destiny in a pattern of battle—be uprooted by thunder and fire!

Scripture: Isaiah 10:27

804.

Let the chains of chronic failure, fear, and delay be shattered beyond repair by the power of the Holy Ghost!

Scripture: Psalm 107:14

805.

I destroy every affliction that resurfaces seasonally—this cycle is broken forever in Jesus' name!

Scripture: Ecclesiastes 3:1

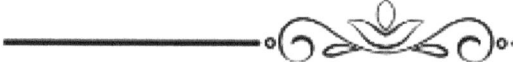

806.

O Lord, send your earthquake into the foundation of every long-term bondage in my life—let the prison collapse!

Scripture: Acts 16:26

807.
Every affliction that has defied medicine, prayer, and fasting—be consumed now by Holy Ghost fire!

Scripture: Exodus 15:26

808.
I release divine thunder against every stubborn situation designed to waste my years—scatter now!

Scripture: Joel 2:25

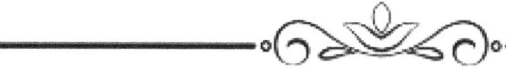

809.
Let every strongman assigned to extend my suffering—be roasted and overthrown by fire!

Scripture: Mark 3:27

810.

I declare war on inherited afflictions—dry up now and release my health, peace, and destiny!

Scripture: Isaiah 53:5

811.

Every stubborn spirit oppressing my body, mind, or family—loose your grip and be bound by thunder!

Scripture: Luke 13:11-13

812.

I pull down every altar sustaining incurable issues—be shattered by the Blood of Jesus!

Scripture: Jeremiah 32:27

813.

I rebuke every foul spirit that keeps reactivating old problems—scatter now in Jesus' name!

Scripture: Matthew 12:43-45

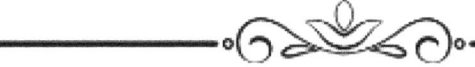

814.

Every demonic time bomb planted in my life to erupt later—be defused and destroyed by Holy Ghost fire!

Scripture: Psalm 11:6

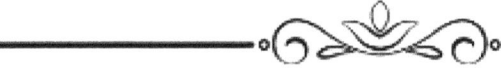

815.

I command every stubborn case in my life to bow at the name of Jesus—no resistance shall prevail!

Scripture: Philippians 2:10

816.
Let every oppression behind closed doors—physical or spiritual—expire by divine judgment!

Scripture: Psalm 34:19

817.
Every witchcraft-induced diagnosis, pain, or torment—reverse now and be buried forever!

Scripture: Matthew 8:17

818.
I declare: No more long-standing limitations—my testimony shall manifest by fire!

Scripture: Isaiah 43:18-19

819.

I release missiles of divine fire into every affliction that has made my name a mockery—scatter now!

Scripture: Psalm 3:3

820.

Let every stubborn wall of resistance break by the blast of Jehovah's breath!

Scripture: Isaiah 30:30

821.

I call forth my healing, breakthrough, and release from every long-occupied bondage—manifest now!

Scripture: Zechariah 9:12

822.
Let every affliction that has become a household name in my family—be silenced permanently by the Blood!

Scripture: Obadiah 1:17

823.
Every root of terminal affliction—be uprooted by the sword of the Lord now!

Scripture: Matthew 15:13

824.
I release fire into every demonic storage room holding my delayed miracles—let it be opened and emptied now!

Scripture: Isaiah 45:3

825.

Every spiritual record of affliction, loss, or oppression—be wiped out by divine mercy!

Scripture: Colossians 2:14

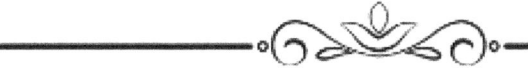

826.

O God, arise and wipe away my tears—turn my battles into breakthrough and songs of deliverance!

Scripture: Psalm 30:5

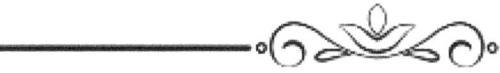

827.

Let divine visitation terminate every case marked as "stubborn" by men—turn it to sudden testimony!

Scripture: Luke 1:37

828.

I declare: My long battle is over—my season of sudden joy, healing, and settlement has begun!

Scripture: Isaiah 60:22

829.

Let every altar that renews stubborn affliction monthly, yearly, or seasonally—burn to ashes forever!

Scripture: Judges 6:25

830.

I decree total judgment and irreversible destruction upon every affliction that refuses to let go—IN JESUS' NAME!

Scripture: Exodus 14:13-14

SECTION TWENTY-NINE: MISSILES FOR DIVINE RECOVERY OF LOST YEARS, VIRTUES & INHERITANCE (PRAYERS 831–860)

Foundation Scripture:
"Thou shalt not suffer a witch to live."

– Exodus 22:18

831.

O Lord, restore every year I have lost to affliction, battles, sin, or manipulation—redeem my time now!

Scripture: Joel 2:25-26

832.

I command my lost glory, virtues, and strength to return by fire—be restored sevenfold!

Scripture: Proverbs 6:31

833.

Every good thing stolen from me by witchcraft, deception, or delay—be restored now by divine vengeance!

Scripture: Isaiah 42:22

834.

Let the angels of recovery locate every spiritual warehouse where my inheritance is stored—release it by fire!

Scripture: Isaiah 45:3

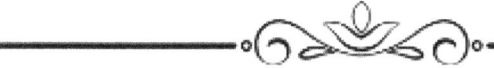

835.

I decree supernatural recall of my divine assignments, gifts, and dreams—let nothing be wasted!

Scripture: Romans 11:29

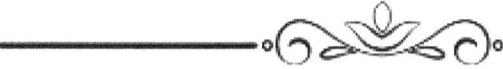

836.

I pull down every spiritual embargo placed on my name, business, ministry, or voice—be lifted now!

Scripture: Psalm 24:7

837.
Let every good thing that was delayed, denied, or diverted—locate me speedily by mercy and fire!

Scripture: Psalm 102:13

838.
I recover every crown, throne, and portion assigned to me before the foundations of the world!

Scripture: Ephesians 1:3-5

839.
Every stolen idea, innovation, or breakthrough moment— be restored to me with divine compensation!

Scripture: Job 42:10

840.
I break the power of spiritual robbers assigned to hijack my harvest—scatter now by thunder!

Scripture: Matthew 13:25

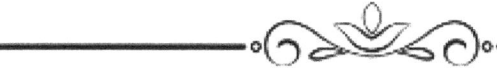

841.
O Lord, let the oil of my head be restored—I walk again in relevance, authority, and dominion!

Scripture: Psalm 23:5

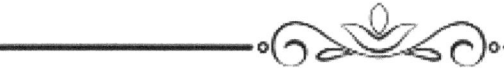

842.
I recall my divine identity from every evil altar where it was buried—resurrect by the Blood of Jesus!

Scripture: Isaiah 43:1

843.

Every prophecy, promise, or word from God that was diverted—be released now by fire and favor!

Scripture: 2 Corinthians 1:20

844.

Let the gates of lost opportunities open wide—I take back what belongs to me in Jesus' name!

Scripture: Revelation 3:8

845

. I receive divine restoration in relationships, ministry, wealth, influence, and legacy—let restoration begin!

Scripture: Jeremiah 30:17

846.

Every demonic calendar marking my delay—be wiped out and replaced with divine speed!

Scripture: Amos 9:13

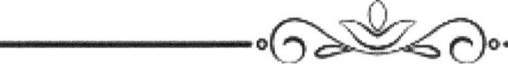

847.

I recover every divine helper that was turned away—let divine reconnection happen now!

Scripture: Psalm 126:1

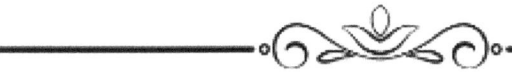

848.

I command the release of my lost virtues held in covens, rivers, or under the earth—resurrect now!

Scripture: Ezekiel 37:12-14

849.
Let the judgment of the Lord fall upon every thief of destiny, time, and health—be consumed without mercy!

Scripture: John 10:10

850.
I recover my place of influence and authority in the spirit realm—let every power bow!

Scripture: Luke 10:19

851.
Every anointing, mantle, or assignment that slipped through my hands—return now in full by mercy!

Scripture: 2 Kings 2:13-15

852.

O God of vengeance, restore what was taken in dreams, dealings, or deception—let justice prevail!

Scripture: Psalm 18:20

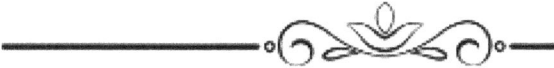

853.

I recall the years, months, and seasons of delay—I recover every divine schedule I missed!

Scripture: Ecclesiastes 3:1

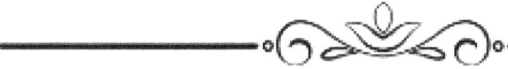

854.

I command my harvest to spring forth without resistance—let restoration answer my sacrifice!

Scripture: Galatians 6:9

855.

Every position, blessing, or office that was diverted from me—be reversed and restored by divine order!

Scripture: Genesis 41:14

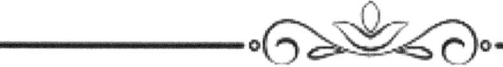

856.

I retrieve every lost fire, passion, and hunger for God— restore my spiritual sensitivity!

Scripture: Revelation 2:4-5

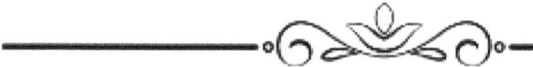

857.

I declare the restoration of prophetic vision, direction, and encounters—my spirit is reawakened!

Scripture: Joel 2:28

858.
Let my stolen inheritance be vomited by every altar or force holding it—no more delay!

Scripture: Job 20:15

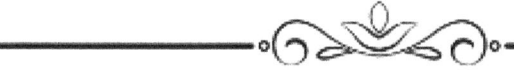

859.
I recall every financial blessing, opportunity, and contract I missed—let divine recall locate me!

Scripture: Deuteronomy 8:18

860.
I declare: My restoration shall be complete, supernatural, and irreversible—IN JESUS' NAME!

Scripture: Obadiah 1:17

SECTION THIRTY: MISSILES TO REVERSE WITCHCRAFT VERDICTS, EVIL COURTROOM JUDGMENTS & DEMONIC LEGAL CLAIMS

(PRAYERS 861–890)

Foundation Scripture:
"Thou shalt not suffer a witch to live."

— Exodus 22:18

861.
Every evil verdict issued against my name in the spirit realm—be reversed now by the Blood of Jesus!

Scripture: Colossians 2:14

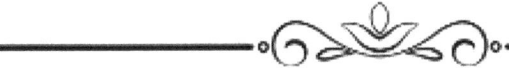

862.
I command every satanic courtroom where my case is pending—scatter now by divine thunder!

Scripture: Isaiah 49:25

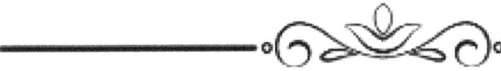

863.
Let every evil judge seated over my destiny be unseated, disgraced, and permanently silenced!

Scripture: Psalm 82:6-7

864.
O Lord, let Your mercy speak and overrule every satanic accusation laid against my life!

Scripture: Romans 8:33-34

865.
I revoke every witchcraft charge filed against me or my household—cancelled by the Blood of the Everlasting Covenant!

Scripture: Hebrews 13:20-21

866.
I plead the case of my destiny before the throne of grace—let divine mercy grant men full acquittal!

Scripture: Zechariah 3:1-4

867.
I release fire upon every lawyer of darkness speaking lies against my elevation—be silenced forever!

Scripture: Psalm 109:2-3

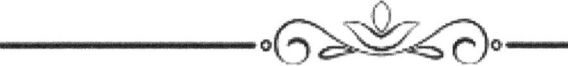

868.
Every witch or wizard who testified against me in a demonic court—be judged and buried by fire!

Scripture: Deuteronomy 19:16-19

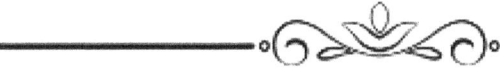

869.
I command every evil gavel that sealed my destiny for delay—be broken by the hammer of the Lord!

Scripture: Jeremiah 23:29

870.

Let the Blood of Jesus override every satanic case file that testifies against my name, voice, or image!

Scripture: Revelation 12:11

871.

O God, tear every veil placed over my life by demonic judgments—let my glory shine again!

Scripture: Isaiah 25:7

872.

I summon angelic advocates to plead my case—let Heaven's courtroom rule in my favor!

Scripture: Daniel 7:10

873.

Every demonic injunction issued to limit my movement, finances, or visibility—expire now!

Scripture: Isaiah 8:10

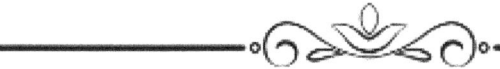

874.

I break every covenant used as legal ground to attack my marriage, ministry, or health—scatter by fire!

Scripture: Isaiah 28:18

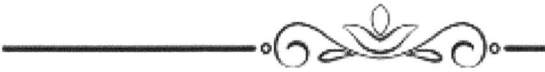

875.

Let the power of the Blood of Jesus nullify every demonic testimony or fabricated evidence!

Scripture: Zechariah 3:3-4

876.
Every spiritual embargo backed by evil documentation—
be torn and erased now by divine intervention!

Scripture: Lamentations 3:37

877.
I decree divine reversal for every witchcraft sentence of
delay, death, or demotion!

Scripture: Psalm 118:17

878.
O Lord, dismiss every court of darkness operating against
my rising and restoration—scatter them by fire!

Scripture: Psalm 2:4-5

879.
I fire missiles of judgment into every ancestral courtroom trying to reclaim my destiny—burn to ashes now!

Scripture: Galatians 3:13

880.
Every false witness who appeared in the spirit to block my blessing—be silenced, exposed, and judged!

Scripture: Proverbs 19:9

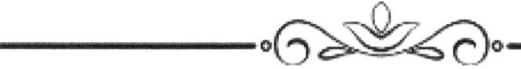

881.
Let every evil altar functioning as a legal system against my family—collapse by thunder and earthquake!

Scripture: Judges 6:25

882.
I erase every spiritual sentence passed against my womb, finances, or testimony—be reversed by mercy!

Scripture: Isaiah 38:5

883.
I declare: No case shall be held against me—I am justified, purified, and exempted by the Blood of Jesus!

Scripture: Romans 5:9

884.
Let the Fire of the Holy Ghost burn every demonic archive where evil rulings were written against me!

Scripture: Psalm 97:3

885.

I declare divine mistrial in every demonic system where my name was unjustly accused!

Scripture: Job 5:12

886.

Every evil judgment written and enforced by sorcery—be torn and replaced with divine verdicts of glory!

Scripture: Psalm 149:9

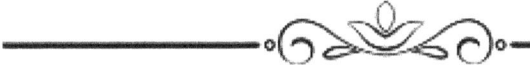

887.

I dismantle every legal altar giving satanic access to my dreams, relationships, or favor—scatter now!

Scripture: Isaiah 54:17

888.
I release divine confusion upon every gathering assembled to prosecute my destiny—scatter by thunder!

Scripture: Psalm 33:10

889.
Let the glory of the Lord shine over every place I was condemned—my story is changing by fire!

Scripture: Isaiah 60:1

890.
I decree: My case is settled, my name is cleared, and my verdict is victory—IN JESUS' NAME!

Scripture: Job 22:28

SECTION THIRTY-ONE: MISSILES TO DESTROY SATANIC MANIPULATION IN RELATIONSHIPS, FRIENDSHIPS & COVENANT BETRAYALS

(PRAYERS 891–920)

Foundation Scripture:
"Thou shalt not suffer a witch to live."

– Exodus 22:18

891.
O Lord, expose and uproot every unfriendly friend positioned in my life as a saboteur—scatter by fire!

Scripture: Psalm 41:9

892.
I break every soul tie with Judas-like figures assigned to betray, delay, or destroy me—be cut off now!

Scripture: John 13:27

893.
Let every relationship I am not supposed to be in—expire now by fire and divine separation!

Scripture: Proverbs 13:20

894.
Every demonic attachment using emotions to manipulate my destiny—be destroyed by the sword of the Lord!

Scripture: Psalm 1:1

895.
I declare: I shall not be manipulated through gifts, guilt, or seduction—Holy Spirit take control!

Scripture: 2 Corinthians 2:11

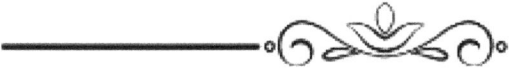

896.
Every evil covenant formed through friendships, conversation, or intimacy—be broken by the Blood of Jesus!

Scripture: Isaiah 28:18

897.
I command the spiritual networks of betrayals assigned to scatter my life—scatter now without recovery!

Scripture: Psalm 55:12-15

898.
Let the sword of God fall upon every relationship draining my virtue—be terminated today by divine judgment!

Scripture: Judges 16:18-21

899.
I revoke every evil agreement I entered into under manipulation or deception—be nullified by the Blood!

Scripture: Colossians 2:14

900.

I speak Holy Ghost fire into every covenant made in darkness, sealed by seduction, lust, or compromise—burn now!

Scripture: Galatians 5:1

901.

Let divine fire expose every secret enemy operating as friend—no more hidden plots, let them be disgraced!

Scripture: 2 Corinthians 11:13-15

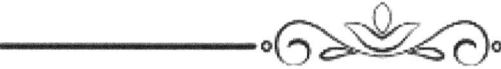

902.

I renounce every false alliance, partnership, or fellowship created to abort my destiny—scatter by thunder!

Scripture: Isaiah 8:10

903.

I disconnect from every manipulative voice leading me away from divine instruction— be silenced now!

Scripture: Romans 8:14

904.

O Lord, deliver me from emotional traps, fake comforters, and masked manipulators—restore my discernment!

Scripture: Proverbs 4:23

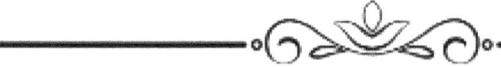

905.

Let fire surround my inner circle—only destiny-aligned people shall remain!

Scripture: Proverbs 27:17

906.
I break every threefold cord of witchcraft, seduction, and betrayal designed to confuse my path—scatter now!

Scripture: Ecclesiastes 4:12

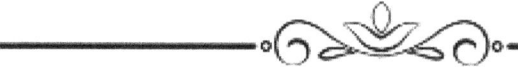

907.
Every voice of witchcraft hiding in loyalty and love—be exposed by divine light and silenced forever!

Scripture: Psalm 64:8

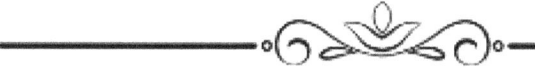

908.
I release divine judgment upon those who swore falsely or dealt treacherously against my progress—let God answer them!

Scripture: Malachi 3:5

909.
Every assignment of emotional manipulation sent to seduce my calling—be cancelled by the power in the Blood!

Scripture: Revelation 2:20

910.
Let every familiar face used to enter my trust and then afflict me—be exposed and removed now!

Scripture: Psalm 55:21

911.
I bind and cast out every python spirit wrapping itself in false compassion—let fire consume it now!

Scripture: Acts 16:16-18

912.

O God, restore every true connection and purify my relationships with fire and truth!

Scripture: John 15:13

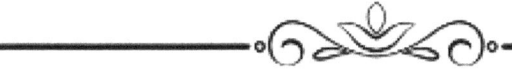

913.

I call forth covenant friendships, divine alliances, and faithful partners for my destiny journey!

Scripture: Ruth 1:16-17

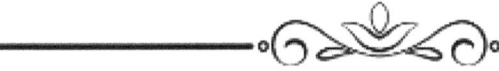

914.

Every word curse spoken during conflict, breakups, or betrayal—be reversed and washed by the Blood!

Scripture: Isaiah 54:17

915.

Every word curse spoken during conflict, breakups, or betrayal—be reversed and washed by the Blood!

Scripture: Isaiah 54:17

916.

I shut down every monitoring voice sent to impersonate help but assigned to harm—be silenced forever!

Scripture: Psalm 34:16

917

Let every soul tie formed in sin, compromise, or ungodly passion—be cut off completely!

Scripture: 2 Corinthians 6:17

918.

I plead the Blood of Jesus over every memory, name, and tie trying to re-enter through manipulation—stay closed!

Scripture: Philippians 3:13

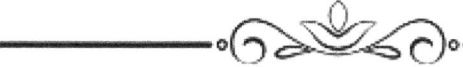

919.

O Lord, purge my inner circle—remove those that have hidden agendas and secret altars!

Scripture: Matthew 7:16

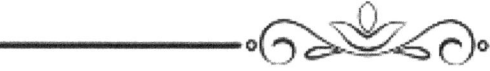

920.

I declare: I am free from all emotional entanglements, manipulative bonds, and deceptive relationships—IN JESUS' NAME!

Scripture: John 8:36

SECTION THIRTY-TWO: MISSILES TO SILENCE TERRITORIAL STRONGHOLDS, REGIONAL THRONES & DEMONIC GATES (PRAYERS 921–950)

Foundation Scripture:
"Thou shalt not suffer a witch to live."

– Exodus 22:18

921.

O Lord, arise in Your power and overthrow every territorial strongman stationed over my region—scatter them by thunder!

Scripture: Psalm 24:1

922.

I speak to the gates of my city, nation, and community—open to righteousness and close to darkness!

Scripture: Psalm 24:7-10

923.

Every satanic throne erected to control regions and destinies—be uprooted and cast into desolation!

Scripture: Jeremiah 1:10

924.
I release fire upon every demonic prince assigned to delay the move of God in my land—be judged and displaced!

Scripture: Daniel 10:13

925.
Let the altar of Jehovah be established over my city—let every evil altar collapse before it!

Scripture: Judges 6:24-25

926.
I call forth prophetic intercession to shake thrones of witchcraft, ancestral worship, and regional idolatry!

Scripture: Isaiah 2:18

927.
Let divine bombs fall upon marine, occult, and political thrones resisting kingdom advancement in my nation!

Scripture: Psalm 2:8-9

928.
I silence every demonic gatekeeper enforcing evil decrees in my environment—be removed by the sword of fire!

Scripture: Isaiah 60:11

929.
O God, send revival wind to sweep through my territory— let every demon lose its grip!

Scripture: Joel 2:28-29

930.

I claim my inheritance in the land—let every invisible barrier to influence and dominion scatter now!

Scripture: Joshua 1:3

931.

I renounce the worship of idols, territorial gods, and cultural bondage affecting my region—let it collapse by judgment!

Scripture: Exodus 20:3-5

932.

Every blood sacrifice speaking in the gates of my city—be silenced forever by the Blood of Jesus!

Scripture: Hebrews 12:24

933.
I take my place as a territorial intercessor—no more witchcraft rulership in my environment!

Scripture: Ezekiel 22:30

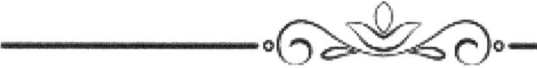

934.
Let angelic armies patrol my city day and night—let evil meetings scatter and demonic plans fail!

Scripture: Psalm 34:7

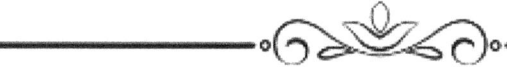

935.
Every unholy alliance between local rulers and witchcraft altars—be exposed and broken now!

Scripture: Isaiah 8:10

936.

I destroy every ancestral claim to the land where I live—only the Lord shall be enthroned there!

Scripture: Numbers 33:52-53

937.

I command the voice of territorial curses to be silenced permanently—let the land yield increase to the righteous!

Scripture: Genesis 26:12

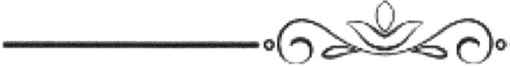

938.

Let the Lion of Judah roar over my nation—scatter occultic councils and evil foundations!

Scripture: Revelation 5:5

939.

Every dark spiritual structure erected over governmental seats, cultural shrines, and political thrones—collapse now!

Scripture: Isaiah 25:7

940.

I reclaim every stolen region, town, and community for the Lord—let light drive out darkness now!

Scripture: Matthew 5:14

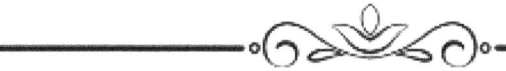

941.

I declare open heavens over my region—every demonic canopy be torn by the wind of fire!

Scripture: Isaiah 64:1

942.

O Lord, possess every gate of commerce, education, and religion—let kingdom takeover begin now!

Scripture: Obadiah 1:21

943.

I scatter every spiritual embargo over church growth, revival fire, and territorial dominion—be lifted now!

Scripture: Matthew 16:18

944.

Let the judgment of God strike every coven that has planted itself near my home, church, or community!

Scripture: Deuteronomy 18:10-12

945.

I command the arrest of every demonic agent working within government, media, or education to suppress truth!

Scripture: Psalm 75:7

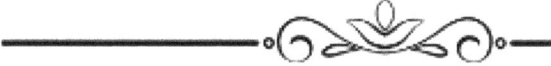

946.

O Lord, shake every altar of Baal, Asherah, and Mammon controlling the systems of this land!

Scripture: Judges 6:28-30

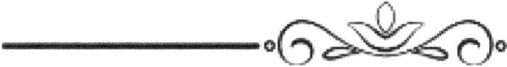

947.

Let the fire of the Lord consume every spiritual gate locked against kingdom influencers—open now!

Scripture: Revelation 3:7-8

948.

I release missiles of warfare into every stronghold of false religion, deception, and antichrist agendas!

Scripture: 2 Corinthians 10:4-5

949.

I declare: My voice shall be heard in my land—my destiny shall influence my territory for Jesus Christ!

Scripture: Psalm 19:4

950.

I decree: The throne of Jesus is established in my nation, my city, and my home—forever and ever!

Scripture: Revelation 11:15

SECTION THIRTY-THREE: MISSILES FOR FINAL VENGEANCE, BREAKTHROUGH & PROPHETIC FIRE SEALING

(PRAYERS 951–1000)

Foundation Scripture:
"Thou shalt not suffer a witch to live."

— Exodus 22:18

951.

I release the fire of vengeance against every witch, altar, and stronghold that refused to let go—scatter forever!

Scripture: Isaiah 63:4

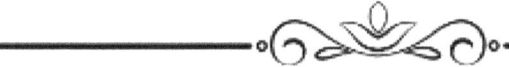

952.

O God of Elijah, arise and settle my case with thunder—let every stubborn enemy bow to Your fire!

Scripture: 2 Kings 1:10

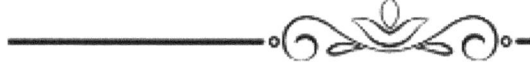

953.

I declare the final judgment upon every evil pursuer—fall like Pharaoh in the Red Sea!

Scripture: Exodus 14:27-28

954.
Every power that has vowed I will never rise—be consumed by divine fury and disgrace!

Scripture: Psalm 68:1-2

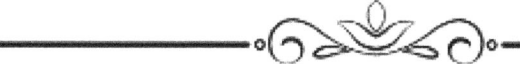

955.
I command prophetic fire to fall upon every altar of delay, backwardness, and affliction—burn to ashes!

Scripture: Leviticus 6:13

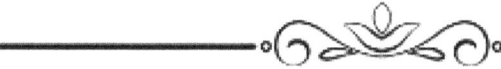

956.
Let the blood of Jesus erase every final accusation from hell—my name is cleared, my destiny is restored!

Scripture: Revelation 12:11

957.
I command sevenfold restoration of everything I have lost—virtue, time, peace, and reward!

Scripture: Proverbs 6:31

958.
Let every prophecy hanging over my life manifest by fire—no more delay, no more hindrance!

Scripture: Habakkuk 2:3

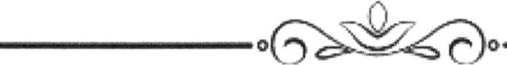

959.
I decree complete turnaround—where there was shame, let glory rise; where there was pain, let power reign!

Scripture: Isaiah 61:7

960.

I reverse every demonic conclusion made over my destiny—I rewrite my story by the Word of God!

Scripture: Job 22:28

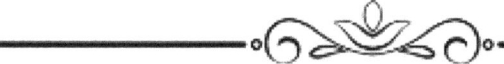

961.

I release my voice into the spirit realm—let every enemy of my voice go silent forever!

Scripture: Psalm 31:18

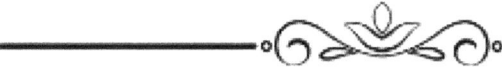

962.

Let the fire of revival ignite my spirit, my home, and my generation—let holy fire never go out!

Scripture: Romans 12:11

963.

I declare: No battle shall rise again—I walk in perpetual victory by the Blood of Jesus!

Scripture: Nahum 1:9

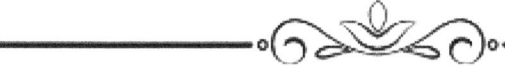

964.

Every battle that followed me from birth—this is your end! Be buried by the sword of the Lord!

Scripture: Jeremiah 1:19

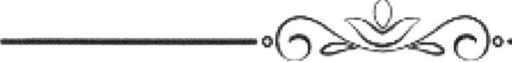

965.

I possess my next level by fire—I step into unshakable breakthrough now!

Scripture: Isaiah 60:1

966.

Let every enemy that resisted me bow to the name of Jesus—total submission and defeat!

Scripture: Philippians 2:10

967.

I declare no more losses, no more near-success failure—I recover all!

Scripture: 1 Samuel 30:8

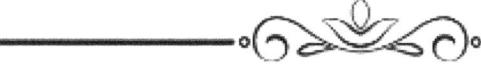

968.

I silence every serpent that still hisses in my atmosphere—be crushed under my feet!

Scripture: Luke 10:19

969.
Every dark cloud over my star, home, or city—scatter by the wind of Jehovah!

Scripture: Isaiah 30:30

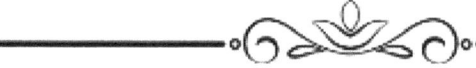

970.
Let the rivers of fire flow through my bloodline—flushing out inherited altars and curses!

Scripture: Malachi 3:2-3

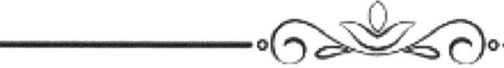

971.
I break into my overflow season—no more stagnation, I possess plenty!

Scripture: Joel 2:24

972.

Let fire go before me and consume every resistance at the gate of my destiny!

Scripture: Psalm 97:3

973.

I call for divine remembrance—let my books of breakthrough be opened now!

Scripture: Esther 6:1-3

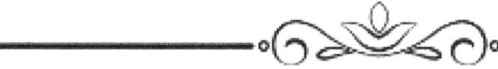

974.

I declare double doors of greatness shall open to me and never shut again!

Scripture: Revelation 3:8

975.

I silence every evil reporter assigned to block my favor—be destroyed by thunder!

Scripture: Isaiah 54:17

976.

Let my enemies bow to the God who answers by fire—Jehovah is my Defender!

Scripture: Exodus 14:14

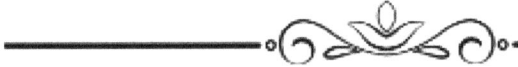

977.

I possess my gates—marital gates, financial gates, ministry gates—by prophetic fire!

Scripture: Genesis 22:17

978.

I declare my spirit is unchained, my future is unlocked, and my future is unchained, my future is unlocked, and my glory is unstoppable!

Scripture: Romans 8:19

979.

Let every altar that rose against me be forgotten forever—I am moving in fire!

Scripture: Psalm 18:44-45

980.

I enter covenant with fire, breakthrough, and open heavens—let new things be born!

Scripture: Isaiah 43:19

981.

Every yoke still hanging around my neck—break by fire, break by thunder, break by the anointing!

Scripture: Isaiah 10:27

982.

I destroy the last root of affliction planted in my family— be plucked up by divine judgment!

Scripture: Matthew 15:13

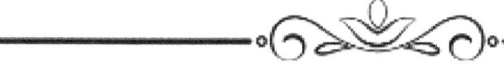

983.

Let the trumpet of my testimony sound in the ears of nations—my season has changed!

Scripture: Psalm 126:1-2

984.

I release the sound of fire—every enemy hiding in the shadows, be exposed and consumed!

Scripture: Ephesians 5:13

985.

I am clothed with garments of fire—sickness, curses, and fear shall not cling to me again!

Scripture: Zechariah 3:4

986.

Every satanic identity placed on me—be erased by fire, I am who God says I am!

Scripture: 1 Peter 2:9

987.
I decree: My voice, my light, my gifts, and my generation shall no longer be silenced!

Scripture: Matthew 5:14

988.
I terminate every satanic cycle with a divine seal—there shall be no re-entry, no return!

Scripture: Nahum 1:9

989.
I walk into divine appointments, supernatural connections, and sudden help from this day forward!

Scripture: Psalm 121:2

990.

I enter my season of prophecy made manifest—what God said, He has done!

Scripture: Numbers 23:19

991.

O Lord, let the world see what You have done—make my testimony loud and unshakable!

Scripture: John 9:25

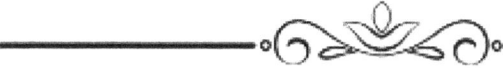

992.

I call forth restoration, restitution, and divine repayment in full—let the thief vomit all!

Scripture: Proverbs 6:31

993.

I decree every attack assigned for my future shall backfire sevenfold—my tomorrow is fire-proof!

Scripture: Psalm 91:7

994.

Let the shadow of death be swallowed forever—I rise in life, light, and divine health!

Scripture: Isaiah 25:8

995.

O Lord, thank You for the fire, the victory, and the fulfillment of Your Word in my life!

Scripture: 2 Samuel 22:31

996.

I seal every prayer in this book with fire and with the Blood of Jesus—no retaliation, no return!

Scripture: Revelation 12:11

997.

I command generational deliverance, revival, and fire to break forth from my bloodline!

Scripture: Acts 2:39

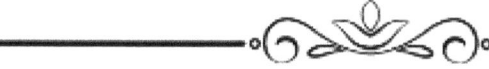

998.

I declare this book is a spiritual weapon—let it produce fire, results, and freedom for all who use it!

Scripture: Hebrews 4:12

999.

I activate every prayer missile in this manual—let them work 24/7 to defend, fight, and empower me!

Scripture: Psalm 18:39

1000.

I declare: I am unchained. I am unstoppable. I am fire-branded. I am victorious. I am a warrior. I am free—IN JESUS' NAME!

Scripture: Romans 8:37

FINAL DECLARATION: I AM FIRE-BRANDED AND UNSTOPPABLE

I declare in the name of Jesus:

I am a warrior of fire.

I am a deliverer in my generation.

I am a restorer of my bloodline.

I am a terror to the kingdom of darkness.

Every missile I have prayed is loaded with power.

Every scripture I have declared is a sword.

Every altar I have destroyed shall never rise again.

I am soaked in the Blood of Jesus.

I am surrounded by angelic reinforcements.

I am empowered by the Word of God.

I am bold, fearless, and unshakable.

From today forward:

✓ I walk in breakthrough.

✓ I operate in dominion.

✓ I carry the fire of God.

✓ I live a life of victory.

This book is sealed. My testimony is permanent.

No power shall retaliate. No witch shall regroup.

I go from fire to fire, from glory to glory.

IN JESUS' MIGHTY NAME. AMEN!

SCRIPTURE SEAL:

"They overcame him by the blood of the Lamb and by the word of their testimony."

– Revelation 12:11

MESSAGE FROM THE AUTHOR

Beloved Warrior,

This book is not ordinary. It was birthed in the place of travail, fire, and relentless warfare. These 1000 atomic bomb missiles were divinely downloaded as spiritual weapons to equip you for the battle that many avoid. We are not praying gentle prayers here—we are declaring war. Witchcraft is real. Evil altars are real. But the power of God is greater. These prayers are not suggestions. They are declarations, decrees, and divine weapons forged by scripture to break chains, burn altars, and release destinies.

This manual is for those who are tired of delay, tired of oppression, and tired of spiritual silence. It is for those who want to see fire fall, breakthroughs manifest, and testimonies overflow. It is for the bold. It is for the desperate. It is for the warrior in you. I encourage you:

Pray at midnight. Fast as the Holy Spirit leads.

Shout when you must. Weep when you must.

But don't stop until something breaks. Pray one prayer 3 times. Or 5.Or 10.Or 15. Or 20. Don't rush. Don't quit. Don't apologize.

You are a firebrand. You are unstoppable. You are dangerous to darkness. Let this book be your battle companion until every altar that ever rose against you is destroyed, and your generation is delivered. With fire and love,

Evangelist Tracy C. Moonga

Healing Minister | Intercessor | Fire-Prophetic Voice | End-Time Warrior

Gospel Songwriter | Worshipper | Revival Sound Carrier

Soul-Winner with a Divine Assignment to Populate Heaven and Depopulate Hell

ABOUT THE AUTHOR

Evangelist Tracy C. Moonga is a fire-branded healing minister, end-time intercessor, and a prophetic voice called to awaken, equip, and set captives free through the power of prayer and the Word. Her personal journey from affliction to divine calling fuels her mission to raise spiritual warriors and ignite revival fire in families, churches, and nations. She is the author of over 50 explosive prayer manuals and declarations, known for her bold delivery, unwavering faith, and uncompromising message. Evangelist Tracy is also a gospel songwriter, worshipper, and revival sound carrier. Her divine assignment is simple but urgent: Populate Heaven and Depopulate Hell. She resides in Australia and continues to minister internationally with fire, conviction, and results.

BOOKS BY EVANGELIST TRACY C. MOONGA

1. 1000 Atomic Bomb Missiles Against Witchcraft and Evil Altars
2. Healing in Advance: 1000 Prayers of Thanksgiving and Faith
3. 2,000 Fire-Packed Thanksgiving Prayers to Crush Sickness and Defeat the Devil
4. Fire-Packed Prayers for Spiritual Warfare, Breakthroughs, and Deliverance
5. Pleading the Blood of Jesus: Fire-Packed Prayers and Declarations
6. 200 Daily Prophetic Personalized Declarations for Healing and Long Life
7. The Psalms Arsenal: 365 Personalized Confessions for Spiritual Warfare
8. Father, I Thank You for Healing
9. Wounded but Not Defeated: Storms Were Meant to Shape You, Not Break You
10. Win a Soul for Christ
11. Single with a Purpose
12. Don't Miss Eternity: The Call to a Meaningful Life
13. Seek God First and These Things Shall Be Added to You
14. Be the Doer of God's Word in Faith
15. Bone of My Bones and Flesh of My Flesh

SHARE YOUR TESTIMONY

Has God touched you through this book?

Have altars been destroyed?

Have you seen healing, deliverance, or a sudden breakthrough?

SHARE YOUR TESTIMONY AND GIVE GOD THE GLORY!

Testimonies defeat the devil and inspire others to rise.

Connect with Evangelist Tracy C. Moonga:

Facebook: Evangelist Tracy C. Moonga

Instagram: @evangelisttracyc.moonga

Email: evangelisttracyc.moonga@gmail.com

www.ingramcontent.com/pod-product-compliance
Lightning Source LLC
Chambersburg PA
CBHW061724070526
44583CB00024B/3001